D0929302

THE AKITA

Gerald and Kath Mitchell

ACKNOWLEDGEMENTS

Brian Pearson, for his help and dedication to detail in the drawings used in this book.
Lynda J. Ross, B.V.M. & S., M.R.C.V.S., our vet, for her help in verifying the chapter on Health.
Wendy and Spencer Bell, for supplying many of the photographs..
The Kennel Club, and especially Brian Leonard and Ian Logan for the registration and statistical information.
Dog World, David Dalton, John Hartley, David Lindsey, Alan Walker.
All our other Akita friends who contributed information and pictures.

We dedicate this book to all the Akitas of the world. May they be caringly loved, truthfully respected, and most of all knowingly understood. For it is in understanding that they will bring the greatest joy and pleasure to their owners and be able to live out their lives in peace, contentment and happiness.

Ringpress Books Ltd
Spirella House, Bridge Road, Letchworth, Herts, SG6 4ET

First published 1990
ISBN 0 948955 11 2

Production consultants Landmark Ltd
Typeset by Ringpress Books
Printed and Bound in Great Britain by The Bath Press

CONTENTS

INTRODUCTION

OUR interest in the Japanese Akita is not so much a hobby, but more of a vocation, for not only do we have the greatest regard for the breed and a desire to preserve its beauty, we are also determined that everyone who becomes involved in Akitas understands the animal itself. The Akita has a complex mind and behaviour patterns that are peculiar to the breed. Its physical qualities are not easy to preserve, for the close-to-the-wild characteristics will always try to take over from the cosmetic improvements we try to achieve in our breeding of the domesticated dog. While it is important to uphold these visual characteristics, this must never be to the detriment of the true Akita temperament which is a vital part of the breed.

This book has been written with the knowledge we have gained during our thirty years in dogs and with the benefit of the lessons we have learnt in our research of the breed. We do not profess to know everything about this lovely animal, much of the fascination remains the quest for further knowledge. But we have tried to cover the most common problems the Akita owner may encounter, although we believe that more often than not, these problems do not relate to the dogs themselves, but to the owner misunderstanding the nature of the breed. Hopefully, this book will provide a reference to help owners care for their dogs, and will lead to a free exchange of information which will help to advance and promote this magnificent breed.

THE AKITA

CHAPTER 1

ORIGINS OF THE BREED

THE Japanese Akita is steeped in history legend and myth, and over the centuries many attempts have been made to discover the dog's true origin. Documentary evidence, cave drawings and excavated bones have come to light and these have been studied in order to piece together a picture of how the breed evolved. Japan's recorded history spans over two and a half thousand years but information about the Akita is sparse and the language barrier creates further difficulties for British researchers. However, there are a number of authors who have based their work on archaeological, zoological, anthropological and ethnological viewpoints, and this, coupled with the documented history and folklore, present a plausible picture.

It was first believed that people migrated to the Japanese Islands around four thousand years ago, but more recent evidence dates back to the Stone Age. Studies of fossils and skeletal remains have proved that there were domesticated dogs from this era. It is not known if these dogs had prick ears and curled tails, but it is generally presumed that they were related to the present Akita dog. By the Bronze Age there were drawings and artefacts in existence, and these portray the distinctive features of the Japanese-type dog.

The breed came to the forefront in the twelfth century when dog-fighting became a popular sport in Japan. In order to create the best competition, the Akita-type dogs were crossed with other breeds to produce a worthy challenger. When the interest in fighting waned, the dogs were again used for hunting and herding. In the 17th century a famous Japanese war lord was exiled to a fortress on the northern Japanese island of Honshu. He was an admirer of fine sporting dogs, and it is said that he inter-bred the Akita and the Russian Laika dog to produce a larger, more powerful dog with a keen spirit. His animals became highly

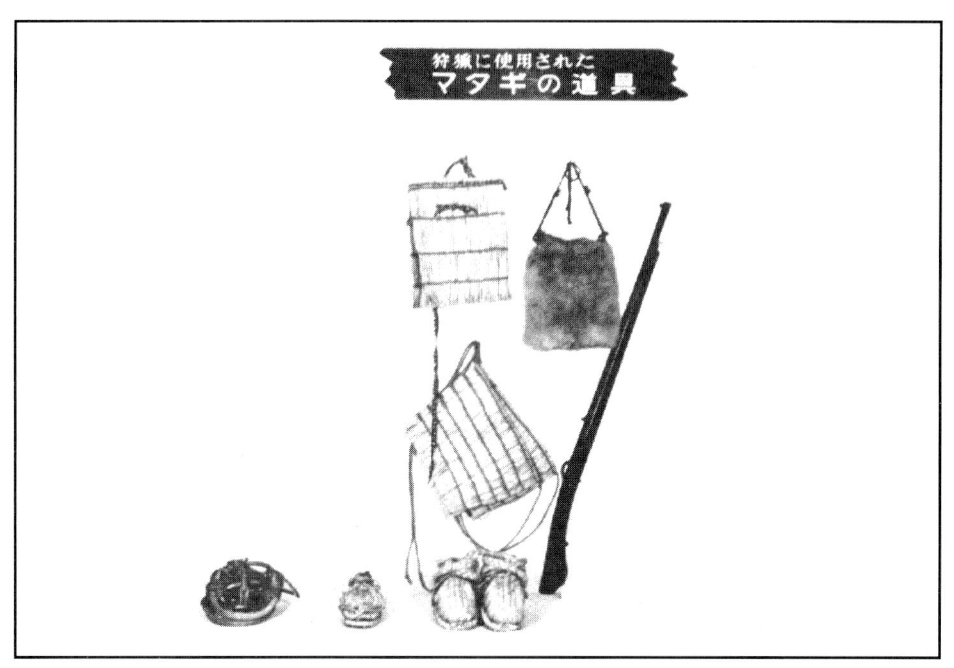

Equipment used when Akitas were employed as hunting dogs.

Skeletons and pelts from Akitas, now on display at the Akita Museum in Japan.

prized among the aristocracy and enjoyed popularity for over a century. Because of the relative isolation of these northern regions, the breed retained a certain purity of type. It is generally believed that the environment had a big influence on the physical characteristics of the breed and the dog's thick coat, strong bones and firm feet probably evolved during this period. Many Akita-type dogs were bred in different areas of Japan, but those from the northern region, known as the Akita Prefecture, were the purest bred and are the true ancestors of the present-day Akita.

In 1899 there was an outbreak of rabies and many dogs had to be destroyed. However, the mountainous terrain of the Akita Prefecture slowed up the spread of the disease, and some dogs managed to survive. In the next few decades dog-fighting became popular again, and this resulted in cross-breeding the Akita with other types, generally the Tosa breed. But famine and starvation meant that once again dogs were in danger, and many were killed for their meat and pelt. Fortunately, there were those who prized the Akita for its intelligence and hunting abilities, and so a number of dogs were bred and used to track and hunt small game such as ducks and other birds, graduating to deer, elk, boar and even the Yezo bear, weighing up to eight hundred pounds. The hunter would set off without a gun, accompanied by a pair of Akitas (one male and one female) which would bring down the prey and hold it until it was either clubbed or speared. The versatile Akita was also used to herd cattle, act as a sight dog, pull loads and work alongside the police. There is documented evidence, found in a Shogunate's hawkchambers, of an Akita type dog working with hawks and falcons. The dogs' webbed feet and thick coat also made them ideal water dogs, and so they often worked with fishermen.

NAMING AND RECOGNITION

In 1927 Mr Shigeie (Mokke) Izumi, the mayor of Odate, capital of the Akita Prefecture, set up the Akita Inu Hozonkai (Akiho) for the purpose of perpetuating true Akita dogs and in 1931 the breed was officially named along with six other Japanese breeds. The Akita Inu, as it was named was declared a natural monument. It was the largest of the Japanese breeds and the Shiba Inu was the smallest. In between came the Hokkaido-Inu, Kosho-No Inu, Kai-Inu, Kishu-Inu and Shikoko-Inu. The city of Odate, on Honshu Island is, still the centre of Akita records and the development of the breed has been meticulously documented.

With official recognition, the breed began to flourish, but this was

The Akiho Headquarters

brought to an abrupt halt during the Second World War. The atomic bomb attack on Hiroshima killed thousands of people and inevitably livestock also perished. The Akita population was drastically reduced, but the ardent fanciers struggled on and in 1948 Akitas were exhibited at the 12th Akiho Dog Show. In 1953 the Akita Preservation Society was established and in 1978, on the fiftieth anniversary of the breed's official recognition, the Akiho Headquarters was built. The record vaults are on the ground floor, a conference suite is on the second level and the Akita Museum, which houses a variety of artefacts, hunting gear and pelts, is on the third floor.

FOLKLORE AND LEGEND

The Akita did not receive official recognition in its native land until 1931, but it has had a special place in the hearts of the Japanese from earliest times. The dog has a mysterious quality, it is highly intelligent, aloof with strangers and yet shows an absolute devotion to its family and would die rather than fail them. The Japanese people prize their heritage and culture, and the Akita has always been associated with good luck and fortune. An

The statue of Hachiko at Shibuyu Railway Station. A special ceremony was held in his memory in 1989, and an Akita was made station master for the day.

The Akita on a Japanese stamp, 1952.
Courtesy of Louise Gadalla

effigy of the Akita is often given at the birth of a baby or to someone who is sick or injured. The breed has been regarded as a status symbol from Shogunate times and it is said that one Shogun owned some four hundred Akitas and kept a special servant to care for each and every one of them. Over the centuries many owners kept the pelts of their most treasured dogs to serve as a lasting reminder, and today the Akita has the distinction of appearing on postage stamps and other official documents. The breed is valued so highly in Japan that if the owner of a champion Akita falls on hard times, the government will pay for the upkeep of the dog for as long as necessary.

Perhaps the most famous Akita of all was one named Hachiko, owned by Dr. Eisaburo Ueno, a professor at Tokyo University. Each morning the dog would walk with his master to Shibuyu railway station to see him off to work, and he would return each day at 3pm to greet him as he returned on the afternoon train. On May 21st. 1925, the doctor left as usual, but he did not return. He had suffered a stroke and died at the university. Hachiko returned to Shibuyu station every day, each morning and each afternoon for the next ten years. Over the years, the people of Tokyo came to know and love this devoted dog, and gave him food and water. Many made a special journey just to feed and pat him, and to be able to say: "I have seen Hachiko." Finally, on March 7th, 1935, the dog was found dead at the station. But he was not forgotten. In 1943 a small bronze statue was erected in the place where he died, at Shibuyu station. Unfortunately, the war effort meant that all statues were confiscated by the government to be melted down for ore, and the statue of Hachiko was lost. However, in 1948 a son of the original sculptor was commissioned to create another statue, and this was placed in the same spot. Today, the spirit of Hachiko lives on, for the statue has become a special meeting place for lovers. The dog has become a legend in Japan and is a symbol of all that is best in the Japanese Akita — a dog that is uniquely loyal to its master.

THE DEVELOPING LINES

The development of the Japanese Akita into the dog we have today began in the Fifties in Japan. During the war years breeding became scarce and the devastation of Hiroshima drastically reduced the numbers of animals. However, the enthusiasts pressed on, guarding their existing stock, and organising their future breeding lines. Two main types emerged and they became recognised as the two main Akita lines — the Ichinoseki and the Dewa.

It is acknowledged that Goromaru-Go was the most important dog in bringing the Akita up to standard after the war. He was a red-and-white pinto puppy with a large head and small, deep-set triangular eyes. The quality of this dog's offspring was greatly admired and he was, no doubt, responsible for all Akitas with the beautiful pinto colouring we see today. The Dewa line developed at the same time and derived its name from the dog named Dewa-Go. His offspring were stately in build, they had a gentle temperament but were firm and loyal when necessary. They did lose some value because of looseness of skin around the throat and on the lips, which were regarded as a departure from the true Japanese dog image. Although offspring of Dewa-Go were noted in the show ring, there is almost no evidence of this line in Japan today. However, examples of his distinctive dark colouring can be seen in other countries.

The present-day Akita in Japan is lighter in build than those which have developed from the combination of of Ichinoseki and Dewa lines in other parts of the world. They have finer head features and are shorter in body, though not in leg length. They excel in coat-colourings and quality and have superb small triangular ears, correctly shaped and set on to the head. Their eyes are clear and noticably free from the eye problems that are sometimes found in other strains. Many examples of true, present-day Japanese Akitas can be found in Europe and Scandinavia, along with a small influence in Canada and Great Britain The Ichinoseki and Dewa strains were both imported into the United States and it is offspring from these combinations that have found their way around the rest of the world and form the base of Akitas in many countries.

CHAPTER TWO

OUT OF JAPAN

THE magnificent physical appearance of the Akita coupled with its loyal, steadfast temperament has ensured the breed's popularity outside its native home. America was the first country to adopt the Akita, and one of the first dogs to emigrate was Kamikaze (Divine Wind), which was given as a gift to Helen Keller. Helen, an American was blind, deaf and mute. She travelled the world teaching others who were similarly afflicted, to lead a fuller life. In the late Thirties she was lecturing in Japan and she expressed a wish to own an Akita. She had discovered the breed's rare quality of being able to communicate through body language. This is something apparent in all dogs, but most Akita owners would agree that the breed is peculiarly sensitive. For someone as severely handicapped as Helen Keller, this extra degree of communication was all-important. An officer in the police force, Ichiro Ogasawara, presented Miss Keller with an Akita in recognition of her work with the handicapped. This was a rare and precious gift, for at this time there were very few of the breed left, save in their northern home of the Akita Prefecture. Kamikaze travelled to America with Miss Keller but became ill when he was only eight months old and died from distemper. In 1939 some friends in Japan sent her another Akita and the dog, Kenzan-Go, remained with Helen Keller until his death in the mid-Forties. In her characteristic gentle style, she referred to her Akita as an Angel in Fur.

The number of Akitas reaching the United States grew rapidly after the Second World War when servicemen who had been stationed in the Japanese Islands took dogs home with them. Some of these imports found their way to dog enthusiasts and these formed the basis for present-day Akitas, not only in America but in Canada, Australia, some European countries, including Scandinavia, the islands off America, Great Britain and its colonies. There were numerous lines of development stemming from these early imports, and these have been well documented. Today the influence of these early pedigrees is minimal and there are just a few old photographs that have survived. Many of the early dogs went to novices who did not understand about breeding livestock, and so lessons had to be learnt. Some did stick with the breed and eventually the numbers grew and some good dogs came to the fore. Breeding lines were established and a specialised club for the breed was set up. In 1955 the American Kennel Club gave permission for the Akita to be exhibited in their miscellaneous class, but it was seventeen years before it was given individual status.

It was comparatively soon after this official recognition that the first Akitas were imported to Britain in 1981. Skilful breeding in the United States had produced Akitas which were strikingly beautiful, and which carried the characteristics of the breed. But because their pedigrees were a mixture of all the early imports, there had not been enough time to remedy all the inherited faults or establish a perfect type. As a result there was a great diversity in the Akitas which arrived in Britain. Some representatives of the breed were exported direct from Japan, and in Scandinavia these formed the basis of their initial breeding stock. But British breeding lines can trace only two dogs which were imported direct from Japan. Language difficulties have prevented a free exchange of information between Japan and countries that breed the Akita, and until recently, no one knew their response to the Western version of the Akita. Certainly, Western breeders have always tried to remain true to the Japanese origins of the breed, even though we have been using Akitas with American pedigrees. But now the latest word from Japan is that breeders are thinking of enhancing their own stock with Akitas that have been bred overseas. The Japanese Akita is certainly becoming an international dog, with many countries now playing a part in its future. Let us hope that the emigration of the breed to other lands will serve it well, and preserve the Akita in its purest form.

CHAPTER THREE

THE BREED IN BRITAIN

THE first Akitas to enter the United Kingdom were a pair imported from Japan in the Forties by a Japanese gentleman with the unlikely name of Mr Smith. They were registered with the British Kennel Club and were exhibited at Crufts. However, they were never bred from and when they died the breed ceased to exist in Britain. The next record is rather less well documented as no registration was ever made, but it seems that a dog was imported into Scotland in the Fifties. His owner could not trace any of the breed and so, again, the Akita died out.

The Japanese Akita really began its existence in Britain during the Eighties. The first to be registered in this era was a bitch called Davos Watakyshi Tomo-Dachi. She was imported from Canada by Miss Marion Sargent, who had been on holiday there visiting her sister. The bitch was registered with the Kennel Club in April 1981. In August the same, year Kosho Ki's Kiki of Kiskas was placed in quarantine. Imported from the famous Kosho Ki kennel in California, she was the first show and foundation bitch of our kennel. The next registration was in July 1982 for a bitch of solid white colouring, Yukihime-Go of Rediviva, which was imported from Japan by Mrs Beryl Mason. We had already arranged to import a male, Kosho Ki's Kai of Lindrick, and he was registered with Mike and Joyce Window in March 1983. In August, a bitch named O.B.J. White Hope was registered by Mrs Meg Purnell and Mrs Gonzalez-Camino. At the same time, we received two more imports from the Kosho Ki Kennel. A bitch puppy named Kosho Ki's Kimono Of Kiskas and a dog, Kosho Ki's Song For Adam OTK at Teldale, had entered quarantine together the previous February. We kept the bitch Kimono but we parted with Song For Adam, though we used him at stud on more than one occasion. In September 1983 a registration was made by Mesdames P. Carpenter (who had previously been Mrs. Purnell and had remarried) and

G. Camino, for another American bitch called Am. Ch. O.B.J. Sachette No Okii Yubi. In the same year litter brother and sister Tacara Sumo of Clear Spring and Tacara Saki of Clear Spring were brought in from America by Mrs Carol Davis. In January 1984 two dogs were registered: Fujimatsu Go, owned by Frank and Dorothy Green, was imported from Japan, and Arrowcreeks Redman of Fire, owned by Pieter and Helen Burke, also came from America. So in this three-year period, twelve Akitas — seven bitches and five dogs — were imported and registered.

EARLY BREEDING

The first litter to be registered with the British Kennel Club was born on November 2nd 1983 and was registered in February 1984. There were six puppies, three dogs and three bitches. The mother was Kosho Ki's Kiki of Kiskas and they were sired by Song For Adam. Just a few days earlier, on October 23rd, a litter was whelped out of the bitch Am Ch. O.B.J. Sachette No Okii Yubi, sired by O.B.J. Aces High, which had been quarantined at the Overhills kennels en route to Australia. The litter, which carried the Overhills affix did not achieve registration until July 1984. Both these breedings were from American stock. But Beryl

Davos Watakyshi Tomo Dachi: Imported from Canada by Marion Sargent.

Kosho Ki's Kiki of Kiskas: Imported from the USA by Gerald and Kath Mitchell, pictured here with Kath.

Mason's bitch,Yukihime-Go of Rediviva produced a litter sired by the Green's dog, Fujimatsu Go, which were all Japanese-type.The puppies were born on 26th December 1983. Marion Sargent's bitch, now jointly owned with Mike Window under the new kennel affix of Tegwani, produced a litter to the Australia -bound O.B.J. Aces High in January 1984, and we produced a second litter from Kiki and one out of our bitch, Kimono, both sired by Song For Adam. In July 1984, the Canadian bitch, Davos Watakyshi Tomo-Dachi, produced another litter sired by Redman Of Fire.

Registrations were now stepping up for imported dogs and bitches, and for litters produced to bitches who had been imported in whelp. Kosho Ki's Toki Hannah came into quarantine and there she produced a litter for us, which included Voodoo Doll, who later made history in the show ring. Mr Frank Cassidy's Littlecreek affix appeared on several registrations for both dogs and litters, and by the end of 1984 ninety registrations of Japanese Akitas had been made with the English Kennel Club. The increase in registration figures, from fourteen in 1983 to seventy-four in 1984, showed that the Akita was set to take off in the popularity stakes. But few could have anticipated the dramatic increase which followed. In 1985 the figures almost doubled, and by the end of 1986 that new figure itself had more than doubled. In 1987 there was another big increase, and in 1988 the numbers held firm. 1989 saw another very large increase, but a change in the Kennel Club's registration system means that the figure cannot be compared accurately with the figures produced in the previous eight years.

AKITAS IN THE MEDIA

The Japanese Akita was quick to attract attention from the media and soon photos and articles were appearing in Sunday papers' colour supplements and women's magazines. Television also showed an interest and Akitas were featured on the lunchtime programme *Pebble Mill at One*. We took part in this, and even though the programme went out live, the dogs behaved perfectly. Akitas were also featured on *The Animal Road Show* and on two editions of the Crufts previews.

The publicity helped to promote, the breed and soon local newspapers joined the bandwagon, reporting on the birth of litters and carrying photographs of the rare, and highly photogenic Japanese dogs. We were involved in much of this early publicity, and we were always very careful to ensure that no wild statements were made about the breed's temperament or the price of puppies. We believed it was vital to report the facts accurately, so the breed was never misrepresented.The specialist dog paper *Dog World* featured the Akita in May 1984 with an eight-page article, and they carried a full-colour photograph of puppies from the first UK registered litter on the front page — the Akita had well and truly arrived on the British dog scene.

THE BREED CLUBS

The best way a new breed can be monitored and promoted in the United Kingdom is by setting up a breed club, supported by all those who are involved in the breed. Inevitably, there are differing views as to the way the breed should be managed, and so setting up a breed club for the Japanese Akita proved to be a difficult task. Regrettably, power, politics and commercialism all played an important part in the initial introduction of the Akita to Britain. There were those who saw it as a magnificent breed, either to own or just to admire. There were those who wanted a dog only because it was rare and rather macho. And there were those who thought Akita puppies could sell for a high price and so they wanted to own the breed purely for the revenue it might bring in. It was therefore not surprising that there were different groups of people, each with their

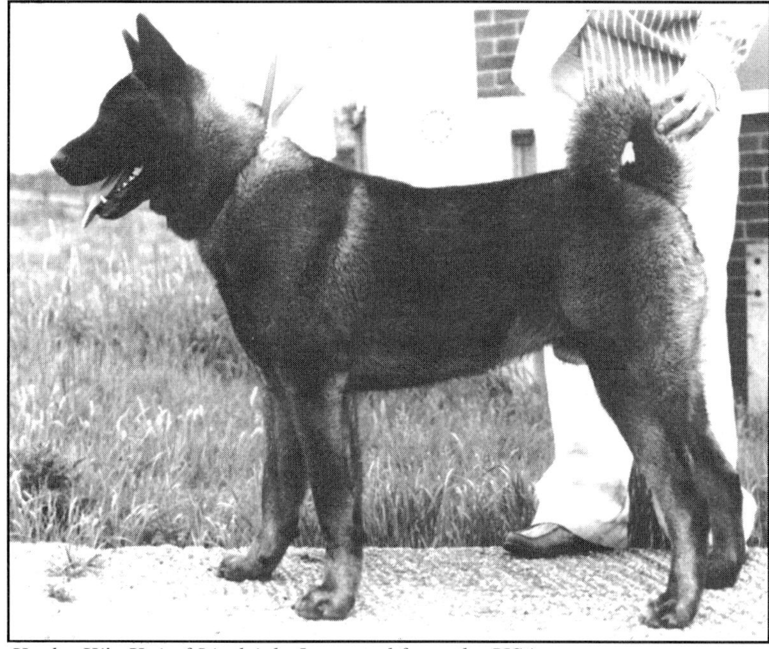

Kosho Ki's Kai of Lindrick: Imported from the USA.

own ideas of how to run a breed club.

January 1983 saw the founding of the first club for the breed, the Japanese Akita Club of Great Britain. This was followed in February 1984 by the British Japanese Akita Society. Three years later in February 1987 the Japanese Akita Association was formed, and the British Japanese Akita Society was disbanded. In September 1988 the Japanese Akita Club of Scotland was formed, serving those who were involved in the breed in the north of the country, although also accepting members worldwide, in common with the other two clubs. So at the present time, the breed is represented by three clubs within the United Kingdom.

BREED EVENTS

The first general Akita event to be held in Britain was the Akita Symposium and Exhibition, in March 1985, which was attended by one hundred and twenty people. This was organised by the Japanese Akita Club of Great Britian and the club also produced an illustrated Akita Guide, which was the first British publication on the Akita. Social functions were held by both the Club and the Society and on October 1st 1988 the first breed club show was held. It was organised by the Japanese

Kosho Ki's Kimono of Kiskas: Imported from the USA.

Kosho Ki's Song For Adam OTK at Teldale: Imported from the USA.

Tacara Sumo of Clearsprings: Imported from the USA by Carol Davis.

Fujimatsu-Go: Imported from Japan by Frank and Dorothy Green.

Arrowcreeks Redman Of Fire: Imported from the USA by Pieter and Helen Burke.

Akita Association, which was now registered with the British Kennel Club. The show attracted an entry of one hundred and sixty five Akitas.

WELFARE AND EDUCATION

As the breed grew in popularity, the health and welfare of Akitas became increasingly important. There was also a need to provide some form of education for Akita judges. In 1988 the Japanese Akita Club of Great Britain set up a 24-hour telephone service called the Akita Hotline. This is the only welfare service in the Akita breed. The privately-run Northern Akita Rescue Service was set up early in 1989 by Gordon and Josephine Brown, to care for and re-house unwanted or abandoned dogs. In the same year the Japanese Akita Club of Great Britain organised two notable events — an Akita Health Conference and an Akita Judges School. The events staged by breed clubs serve as an important meeting place where those involved in the breed can exchange views. The clubs work monitoring the breed and developing welfare and education programmes is essential for the future of the Akita. Every Akita owner should become a member of a club in order to keep up to date with developments, and to share experiences which will lead to a greater understanding of the breed.

The Japanese Akita has not enjoyed an easy introduction into the United Kingdom. It has been the subject of over-breeding, mass advertising and strong marketing, as well as being thrown into the centre of the political arena. But it has attracted many dedicated fanciers, and it is as a result of their hard work and vision that the beautiful Akitas of Great Britain have evolved. Hopefully their dedication, combined with the enthusiasm of newcomers to the breed will steer the Akita to a safe and secure future.

CHAPTER FOUR

THE BREED STANDARD

AS with every pedigree dog, there is a written breed standard for the Japanese Akita. However, in this instance the breed standard is a matter of debate, for there is more than one. The Akita in the UK mainly took its origins from Akitas bred in America, and so they have the look of the dogs living there. These are different in type to today's native Japanese Akita and so the breed now has distinctive types, depending on where the dogs were bred. This is a peculiar situation and it is a cause of some regret that this Japanese breed should be divided into two categories. However, there is no doubt that the Americans have been influential in creating the Akita as it looks today, not only in their own country but in Britain and in many others around the world.

It seems logical to accept that the Akita is either of the Ichinoseki-type or the Dewa-type, although the Americans did change their original Dewa and Ichinoseki line imports, by select breeding and by mixing the two lines to enhance the colouring, style and substance of the Akita. A good American Akita will be very smart and striking, with an aura of class and panache. In contrast, the Japanese have concentrated on producing dogs with a smaller, lighter build. They certainly excel in breeding Akitas with small ears, and with coats of quality and clarity of colour. They have excellent feet and eyes which are are very oriental, and also free of problems.

The British, as one old dog man once said, can take any animal if it is a thoroughbred, and develop it to produce a superb representative of its particular breed. This is becoming the case with the British -Japanese Akita. The breed has developed from its American-born parents and grandparents and has become more refined. British breeders are not so impressed by size and bulk; they tend to prefer good substance and all-round soundness with pronounced masculinity in the males and and a noticeable prettiness in the females. This is reflected in the British Kennel Club standard, which is a mixture of the original standards from Japan and America. Its interpretation of the breed is middle-of-the-road, and this reflects the dogs that most British breeders are trying to produce.

WHY HAVE A BREED STANDARD?

This has proved to be the only way that the individual characteristics of the breed can be codified. It is not enough to breed dogs in the hope that they will look as much like their parents as possible. It is necessary to assess the originals of the breed and record, word by word, the most important characteristics. Inevitably these would be selected from a number of dogs, for the perfect specimen has yet to be produced.

The written standard attempts to create a picture of the the dog and also describes its gait and temperament. But it is essential to examine the dogs in the flesh, in order to interpret the written standard correctly. It should also be accepted that people will interpret the words slightly differently. Beauty is in the eye of the beholder, and the owner of any loved Akita will believe that their dog sums up the standard. However, whatever the individual interpretation may be, the written standard highlights those characterisitics which are absolutely essential in the make-up of a true Akita.

THE KENNEL CLUB BREED STANDARD

GENERAL APPEARANCE: Large, powerful, with much substance and heavy bone.
CHARACTERISTICS: Large broad head, with relatively small eyes and erect ears carried forward in line with back of neck; large curled tail, in balance with head.
TEMPERAMENT: Dignified, courageous, tends to show dominance over other dogs.
HEAD AND SKULL: Skull large and flat, forehead broad, with defined stop and clear furrow. Head forms blunt triangle when viewed from above, free from wrinkle. Cheeks well developed, bridge of nose straight. Nose large and black. Lips tight and black. In white dogs flesh colour is permissible. Muzzle broad and strong.Distance from nose to stop is to distance from stop to occiput as 2-3.
EYES: Relatively small, almond-shaped, clean, moderately set apart and dark brown. Eye rims dark and tight.
EARS: Relatively small, thick, triangular, not low set, carried forward over eyes in line with back of neck and firmly erect. Moderately set apart and slightly rounded at tips.
MOUTH: Jaws strong with perfect, regular and complete scissor bite, i.e.

the upper teeth closely overlapping the lower teeth and set square to the jaws.
NECK: Thick and muscular, comparatively short, widening gradually toward shoulders. Pronounced crest blends with back of skull.
FOREQUARTERS: Shoulders strong and powerful, moderately laid back.Elbows very tight. Forelegs well-boned and straight when viewed from front. Pasterns slightly inclining forward.
BODY: Longer than high, as 10 is to 9 in males, 11 to 9 in bitches. Chest wide and deep, depth of chest is one-half height of dog at shoulder. Well-developed forechest. Level back with firmly muscled loin and moderate tuck-up. Skin pliant but not loose.
HINDQUARTERS: Strong and muscular with long, well developed thighs and moderate turn of stifle. Strong hocks with only moderate angulation, well let down, turning neither in nor out.
FEET: Thick, well-knuckled and very tight turning neither in nor out. Pads hard. Nails hard. Dew claws on hind legs customarily removed.
TAIL: Large and full, set high and carried over back in a three-quarter, full or double curl, always dipping to or below level of back. On a three-quarter curl, tip drops well down flank. Root large and strong.Tail bone

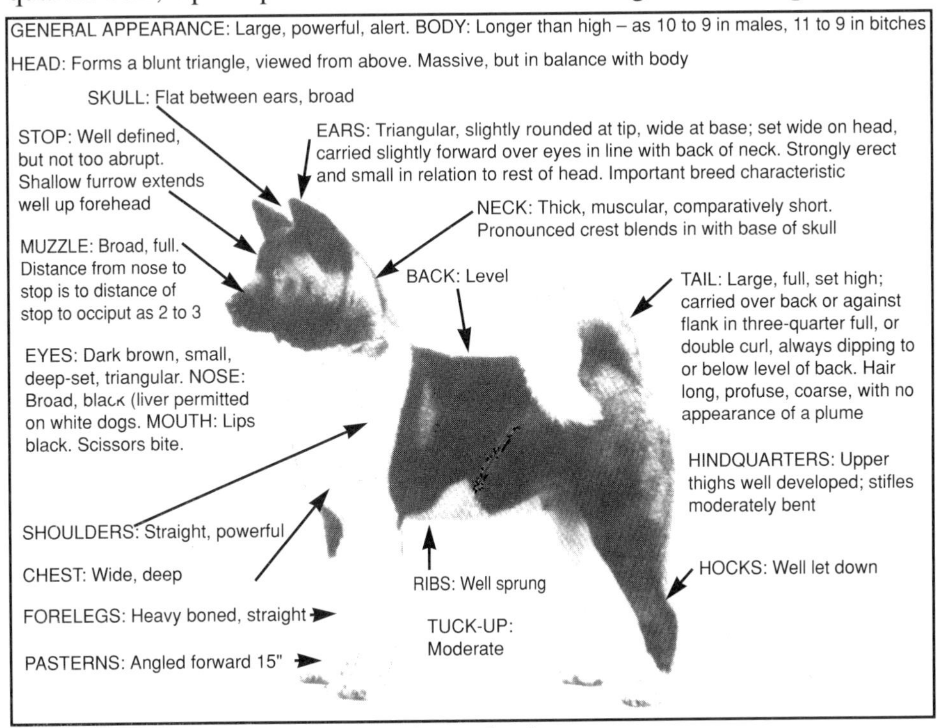

Female Akita typifying the breed standard

almost reaches hock when let down. Hair coarse, straight and full with no appearance of a plume. Sickle or uncurled tail highly undesirable.
GAIT/MOVEMENT: Resilient and vigorous with strides of moderate length. Back remains firm and level. Hindlegs move in line with front legs, whilst gaiting will single track.
COAT: Outer coat coarse, straight and standing off body. Undercoat soft and dense. Coat at withers and rump is approximately two inches and is slightly longer than on rest of body, except on tail where it is more profuse. No indication of ruff or feathering.
COLOUR: Any colour including white, brindle or pinto. Colours are brilliant and clear. Markings are well defined with or without mask or blaze.
SIZE: Height at withers: Dogs 66-71cms(26-28ins); bitches 61-66cms(24-26ins).
FAULTS: Any departure from the foregoing points should be considered a fault and the seriousness with which the fault should be regarded should be in exact proportion to the degree.
NOTE: Male animals should have two apparently normal testicles fully descended into the scrotum.

The Akita should always appear to be a large dog. It is often described as being at the small end of the large breeds' scale, rather than at the top end of the middle-sized breeds. It should therefore never look small or weak; equally it should not appear overdone and coarse in its make-up or expression. The standard refers to a distinctive appearance and these two words describe perfectly the quality required to make a real Akita. The breed has to be distinctive, otherwise it would be just another large Spitz dog with prick ears, a curly tail, and some sort of colouring. Ask yourself this: What are the characteristics of the Bulldog? You will know the answer immediately, for it is those well-known and unique characteristics which makes the Bulldog a Bulldog and not anything else. And so it is with the Akita.When you look at an Akita, it should shout Akita and nothing else.

THE SIX UNIQUE CHARACTERISTICS OF THE BREED

1. The forward-pointing ears of the Akita are an absolute must. They add to the alertness of stance and were almost certainly useful in hunting. They should be small, thick and representing an equilateral triangle in shape.
2. The eyes should be of oriental suggestion, not bold or piggy, but keen

and dark to suggest the "oriental gaze".
3. The beauty and power of the Akita is very much evident in its forward quarters. The shortish, powerful neck should blend almost undetectably into the shoulders: it should only be noticed by the lovely arch which continues into the line of the ear to give that unique, proud stature.
4. The Akita tail is prized by the Japanese people and is considered as important as the head.The tail should be alive and well-carried, to be in perfect balance with the head.
5.The coat should have no suggestion of a wiry or yak-like texture. It should look and feel as though it could be found on that other lovely animal, the mink.
6.The colour is described as brilliant and clear. In the dictionary, 'brilliant' is defined as: splendid, sparkling, shining; and 'clear' is listed as: undimmed, pure and bright. These qualities should be reflected in the colour of the Akita' s coat. It should never be mushy, sooty, dull or lack lustre. Ask the simple question: What colour is that Akita? If you can answer with a definite red, black, silver, fawn etc., the colouring is correct. If you have to say browny, fawny, greyish, sable, creamy-whitish, the colouring is incorrect to the standard of the breed.

The ears, the oriental eye, the line of neck, the high-flung tail, with a most luxuriant and brilliantly coloured coat, are the qualities which capture the Akita fancier's imagination. They are a most definite part of the breed's standard and must be observed intently when breeding so that they are preserved for the future.

THE HEAD MARKINGS

The Akita carries various head markings which are acceptable to the standard. The head may be: all black; self-coloured (the colour being the same as the rest of the dog); coloured as the dog with black mask, (which can extend on to the muzzle and to the stop, or can cover the whole face, i.e. to the stop and out to the cheeks); or masked with white blaze. The blaze can be: either just a small triangle, wide at the nose and narrowing to the stop; wide at the nose, narrowing to the stop, but continuing up on to the skull between the eyes and widening again on the forehead; or just a fine, white pencil line. It is generally accepted that the blaze on an Akita should not be as wide as that of a Spaniel and ideally should end at the stop. White Akitas have no mask. An off-centre blaze or a broad Bull Terrier-type blaze would generally be regarded as a mis-mark and certainly would not enhance the expression of the dog.

Self-coloured: No mask and no blaze.

Black mask, triangular blaze.

All black.

Black mask, narrow pencil-line

THE BODY MARKINGS

THE Akita may be a solid colour (any colour), two colours i.e. one definite colour and white) or pinto (strictly defined as white with colour

Irish-spotted

Pinto

Pinto

Colour and white

Solid colour

patches, evenly placed to cover at least one third of the body). However, it is generally accepted that any Akita which has white colouring in the main, with a coloured head – with or without a mask – and at least one patch of colour, would be called a pinto. A white-coloured Akita that has no colouring, except on its head would be regarded as a mis-mark by many people. A coloured Akita with white socks, with collar, white chest and white tail would be referred to as Irish spotted, which is a genetic term for these markings. An Akita with black colouring, white socks , chest and tail, would be described as black and white, not pinto. An all-white Akita is produced from different genes to those which produce pintos.

THE BODY

The body of the Akita is most important. The proportions for males are nine high to ten long; the females should be nine high to eleven long. The overall impression should be one of just off-square. The chest should be wide and deep, reaching just to the elbow when the dog is mature. It is most important to understand that the Akita is a leggy breed. There should never be any suggestion of short legs, and care must be taken to recognise

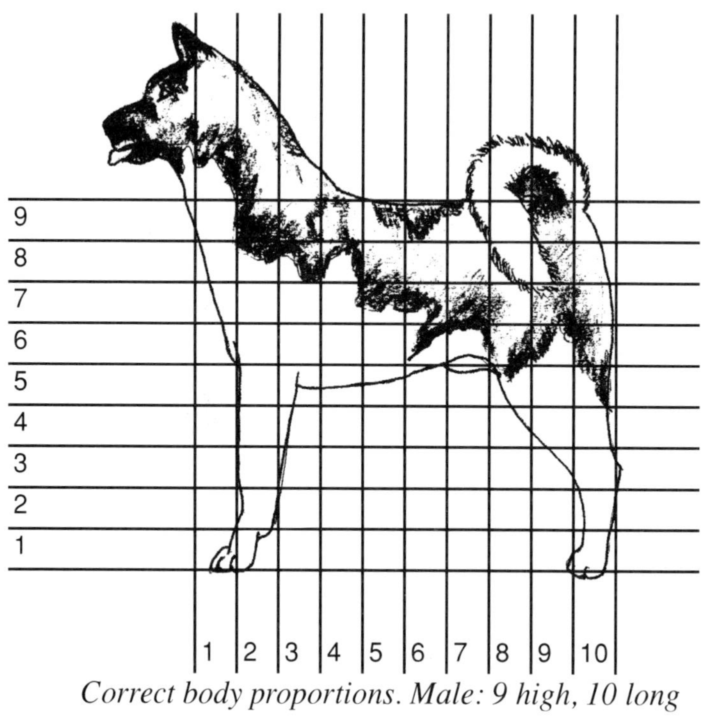

Correct body proportions. Male: 9 high, 10 long

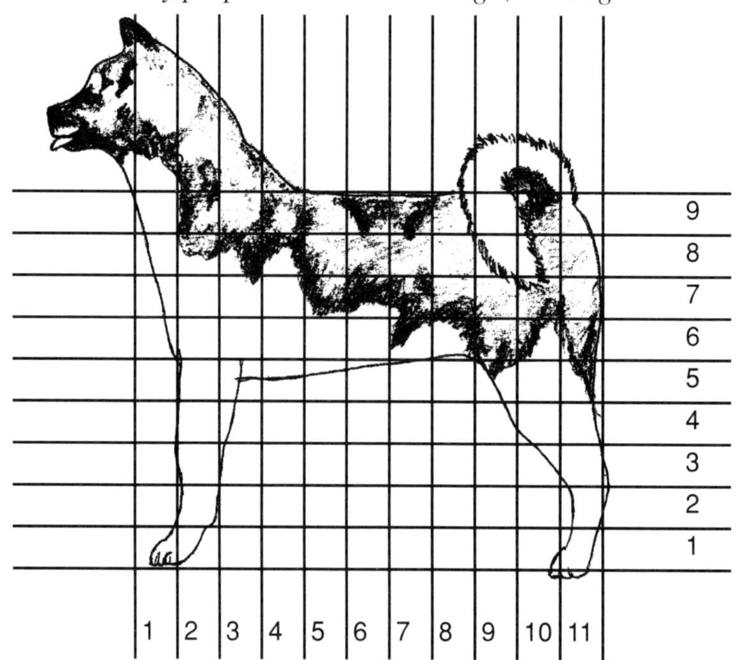

Correct body proportions. Female:9 high to 11 long.

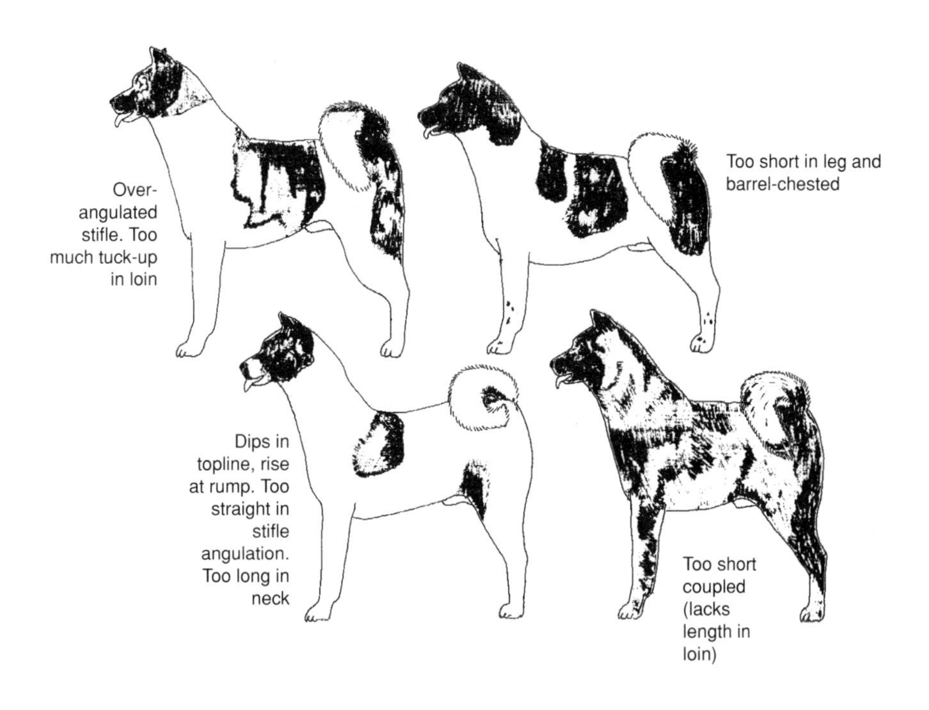
Over-
angulated
stifle. Too
much tuck-up
in loin
Too short in leg and
barrel-chested
Dips in
topline, rise
at rump. Too
straight in
stifle
angulation.
Too long in
neck
Too short
coupled
(lacks
length in
loin)

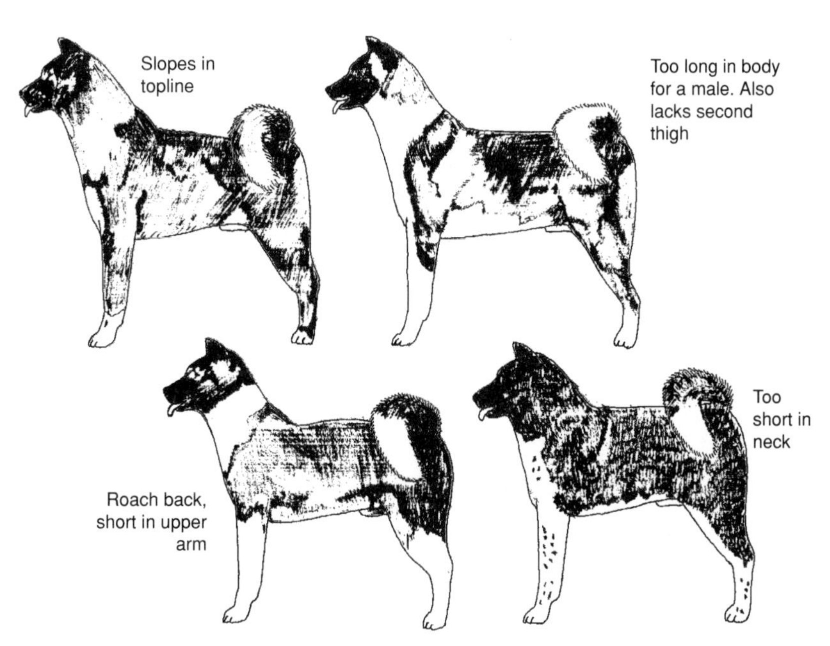
Slopes in
topline
Too long in body
for a male. Also
lacks second
thigh
Roach back,
short in upper
arm
Too
short in
neck

Body faults

this and not confuse the correct proportions with the exaggerated stocky appearance that short legs can often bring. A dog that is too long in the leg is more easily recognisable, and this would also be regarded as a fault. The loin should be strong and firm, the forechest should be well-developed, but not wide or loaded, and the back should always be perfectly level, whether the dog is standing or moving. A rising at the rump or dipping behind the withers would be against the standard, and would be unsuitable for the dog's stature and for its work. A most important characteristic is the tuck-up. This should be so moderate as to be hardly noticeable. In order for the dog to have the strength it requires, the body should be deep and powerful. A shelly, racy body with narrow ribs and pronounced tuck-up cannot fit the standard and does not display the distinctive general appearance of the breed.

THE FRONT OR FOREQUARTERS

These should also be strong and powerful. The shoulders should be only moderately laid back, but they must be laid back and not upright. The upper arm should be in proportion in order to keep the straight legs correctly laid to the shoulder blade so blending in with the neck. Bones should be strong and straight. Pasterns almost upright (at about 15 degrees). Feet should turn neither in nor out, and elbows should be tight into the body.

THE REAR OR HINDQUARTERS

Again strong and muscular, for this is a powerful dog. The loin and upper thighs should be well-developed, and the second thigh should be very much in evidence. This is an area where many fail. The stifle should always be moderately bent — never straight or over-angulated. Hocks should be well let down and the quarters should be wide. Again, feet should point straight ahead.

THE HEAD

This is one of the most important features of the Akita. It should be viewed as a blunt triangle from above, with a large, flat skull and broad forehead. The well-defined stop, clear furrow and broad, deep muzzle all make up a typical picture. The eyes should be set in an oriental fashion and the ears should be placed on the corners of the head – that is to say, neither too far on top of the head nor too much out at the side, which

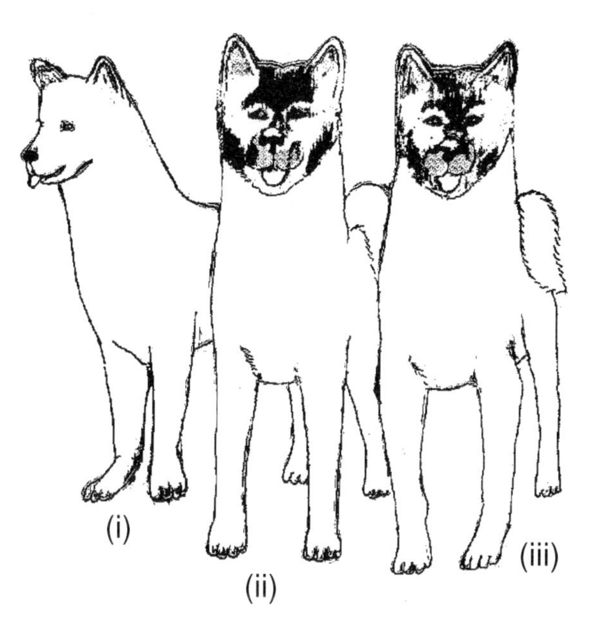

FRONT AND FOREQUARTERS: (i) Narrow-chested and weak pasterns. Poor feet. (ii) Correct. (iii) Out at elbow and toeing in.

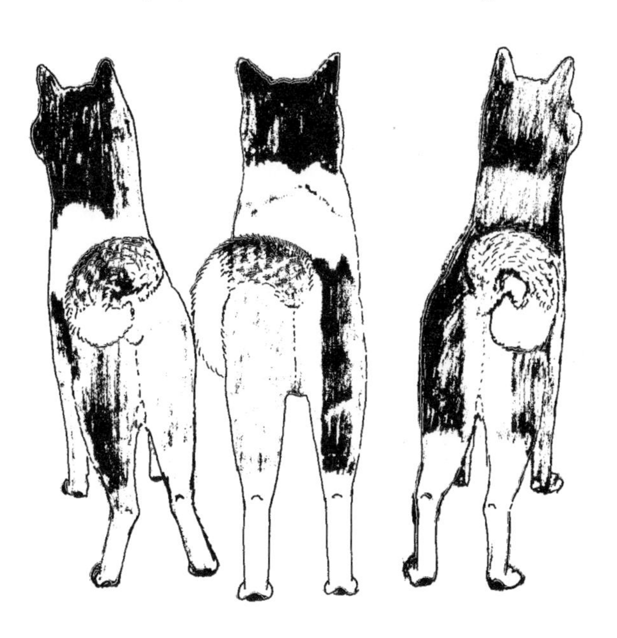

REAR AND HINDQUARTERS: (i) Cow hocks (2) Correct (iii) Weak hocks and feet turning out.

THE HEAD: Correct proportions of the Akita head, ears, eyes and muzzle.

THE HEAD: Good profile head showing correct ears and carriage, good muzzle depth, broad forehead, cheeks and thick, crested neck.

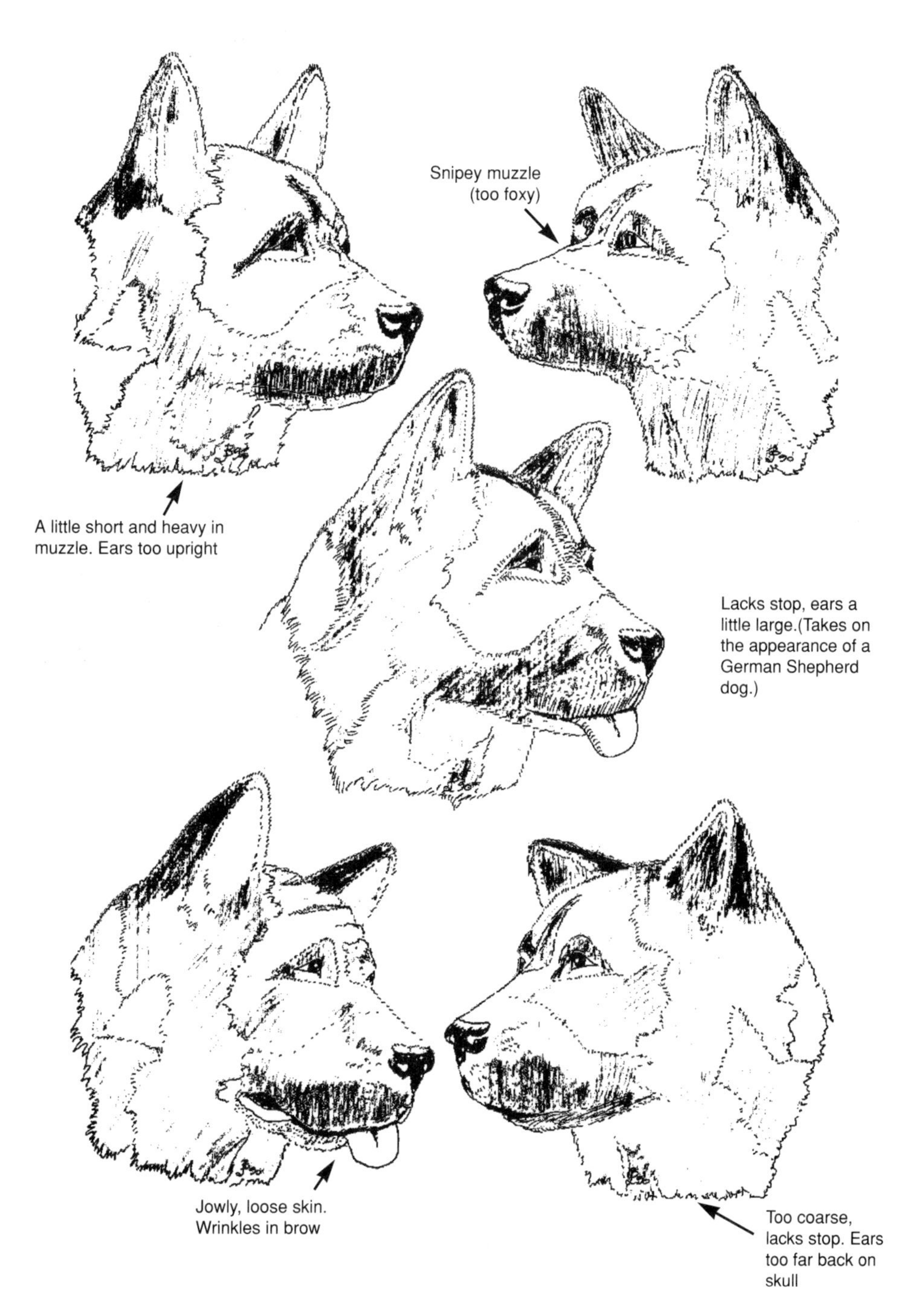

THE HEAD: Various faults

would give a bat-like appearance. Cheeks are required, and they are important for they add to the size of the whole head, but there should not be any loose, jowly flesh or wrinkles. The head should never appear gross or coarse, neither should it be snipey or weak-looking. It should always appear as a powerful, pleasing and well-chiselled picture. Someone once described the Akita head as "a symphony of triangles" – a very fitting analogy.

THE EARS

These have already been specified as one of the unique characteristics of the breed. Without the small, triangular, thick ears, correctly set and angled forward, you have not got an Akita. Not all breed standards mention that the ears should be wide at the base. This is a most important part of the ear. It is essential to have a wide base, correctly set on to the head across the corner, with the eye placed almost in the middle set, creating an oriental slant. There are many breeds with triangular ears, firmly erect. But the Akita must have the correct ear to be synonymous with the breed. The ear should be measured for correct size. This should be done by bringing the tip down to meet the upper eye-rim. It should not

EARS: Left — too far apart. Right — too upright

go any further. Ears set too wide on the head will detract from the keen expression, which is so typical of the breed.

THE EYES

As with any breed, the eyes play an important part in the overall expression. They should be almond-shaped, dark brown (not black), and set in an oriental fashion. The eye rims should be dark and tight. The haw should not show, and there should be no sign of either entropion or ectropion. The eye should never be yellow or light in colour, for it would be a great hardship in the natural environment and would not give the true, intelligent expression. The eyes of the Akita can say a thousand words with one look, and yet can display no intention or thought to a stranger.

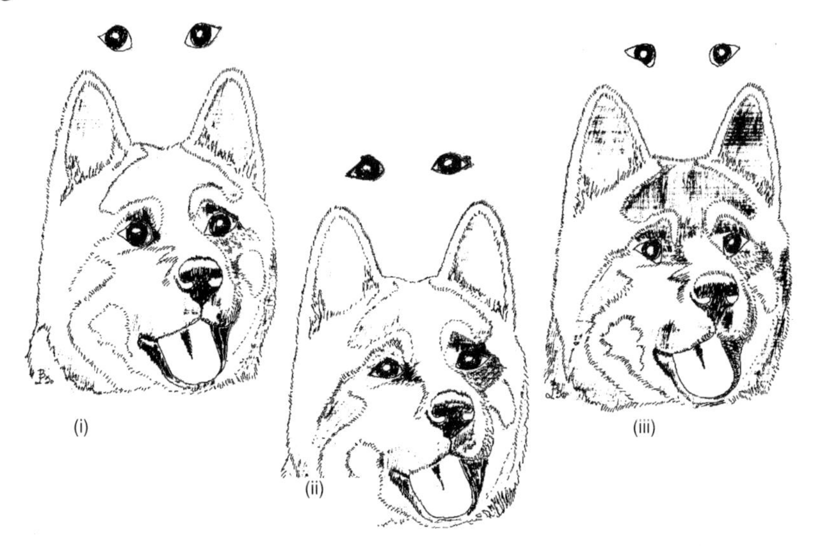

EYES: (i) Too round. (ii) Correct. (iii) Droopy, bad shape and set.

THE MUZZLE

This is an important part of the head and it should be broad, strong and deep. It should not be wide and coarse, nor narrow and snipey. The depth is important and the muzzle should always be checked from the side view to note this quality. The proportions are important: the distance from nose to stop is to the distance from stop to occiput as 2 is to 3. (Do not confuse this proportion 2 to 3 with the proportion of one third to two thirds. They are not the same.)

THE TEETH

The jaws of the Akita are strong and powerful. A complete dentition of forty-two teeth is required and the dog should have a perfect scissor bite i.e. the upper teeth closely overlapping the lower teeth and set square to the jaws. The teeth appear relatively small, for their great roots are deeply embedded in the jaw bones. As the Akita is essentially a hunting and guarding dog, it follows that a proper set of teeth is required. You will occasionally come across an Akita with missing teeth and occasionally one with a level, or maybe even an undershot bite. The standard is quite clear in its demand for a full dentition with a scissor bite and makes no allowances for any other, so therefore any abnormality should be noted.

	name	I	C	P–M	M	sum		
top	*L*	3	1	4	2	10	20	Total number of teeth
	R	3	1	4	2	10		
lower	*L*	3	1	4	3	11	22	
	R	3	1	4	3	11		
	sum	12	4	16	10	42		

I = incisors; C = canines; P–M = pre-molars; M = molars

(i) (ii) (iii)

TEETH: (i) Undershot. Incorrect. (ii) Scissor bite. Correct. (iii) Overshot. Incorrect.

THE TAIL

This is another unique characteristic. It should be alive, full of vigour and vitality and in complete balance with the head. It should be covered with hair, slightly longer than that on the rest of the body. The set should be high, and the tail may fall in a three-quarter, full or double curl, always

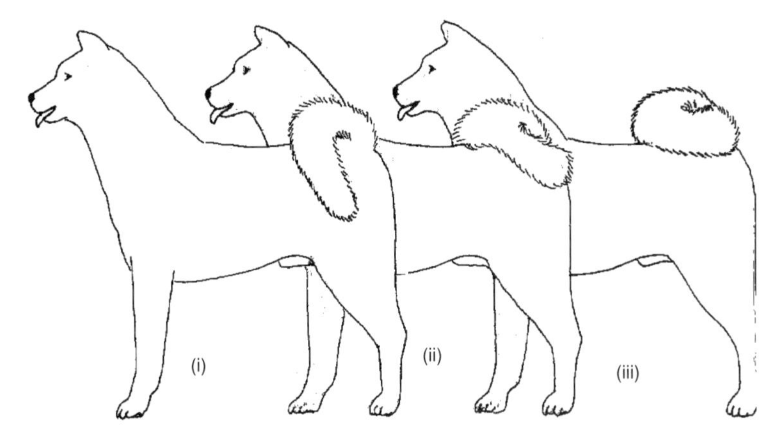

THREE GOOD AKITA TAILS: (i) Tail falling down the flank. (ii) Three-quarter curl. (iii) Full curl. These three typical tails all fall below the level of the topline. All have a thick root . All are set high. All show the correct amount of hair for the plume. Note that no daylight can be seen through the coil.

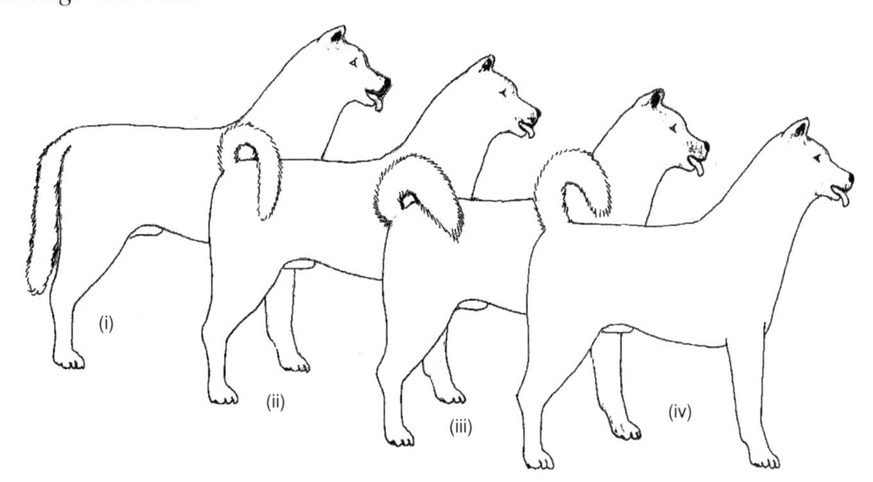

INCORRECT TAILS: (i) Dropped, uncurled. (ii) Thin root, weak tail, lacks plume. (iii) Low set, poor curl. (iv) Sickle. (A disqualification in some breed standards.)

dipping to or below the level of the back. The root should be large and strong, and should always be examined for this quality. A weak, low-set tail does nothing for the stance of the breed. The tail should be carried proudly when on the move or standing. The length should be sufficient to just reach the hock bone when let down. A sickle or uncurled tail is highly undesirable.

THE FEET

The Akita is a very heavy dog and so it needs good strong feet to support itself.These should be thick, well-knuckled and very tight,not turning in or out, with hard, resilient pads and strong nails.

Shallow  *Correct*  *Splayed*

THE COAT AND COLOUR

Perhaps the finest attribute of the breed, the outer coat of straight, harsh hair should be brilliantly coloured and should glow with a translucent effect. The soft, dense undercoat should feel comfortable and will give that plushy, quality appearance which every Akita should have. The length is ideally around one to one and a half inches, although slight deviations from this can still give the correct appearance. Long-coated Akitas do occur but they are generally not suitable for exhibition. Any colour is permissible, provided it is definite, brilliant and clear. Markings should be well defined, that is to say the colours should be clearly separated. There should be no suggestion of various colours mingling or running into each other. The head may be with or without mask or blaze.

GAIT / MOVEMENT

The action should show power and ease. There should be no exaggerated reaching in front or exaggerated driving behind. There should be no mincing, but rather a purposeful stride showing agility and comfort of movement. Think of the shire horse. He is large, powerful and heavy, yet he moves with grace and an ease that belies his great weight. And so it is with the Akita. A smart, medium-striding action is what is required. The front and rear views should be of parallel legs moving in line. The side should show a perfectly level topline and a trotting gait, with no pacing.

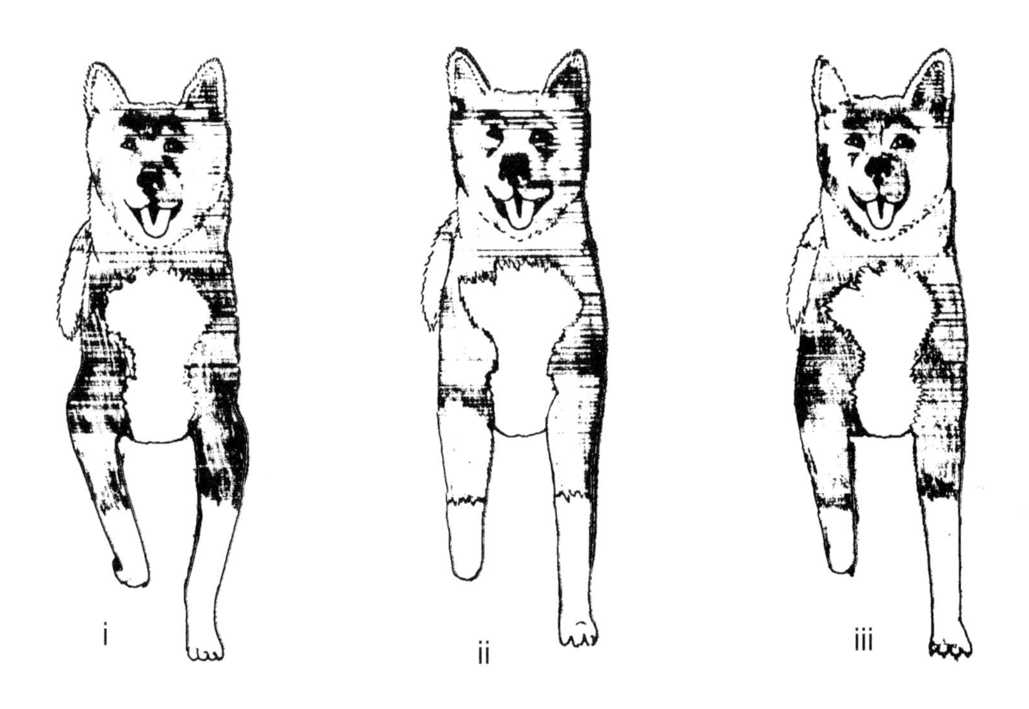

FRONT MOVEMENT: (i) Out at elbow, weak at pastern. (ii) Correct. (iii) Too wide, splayed feet.

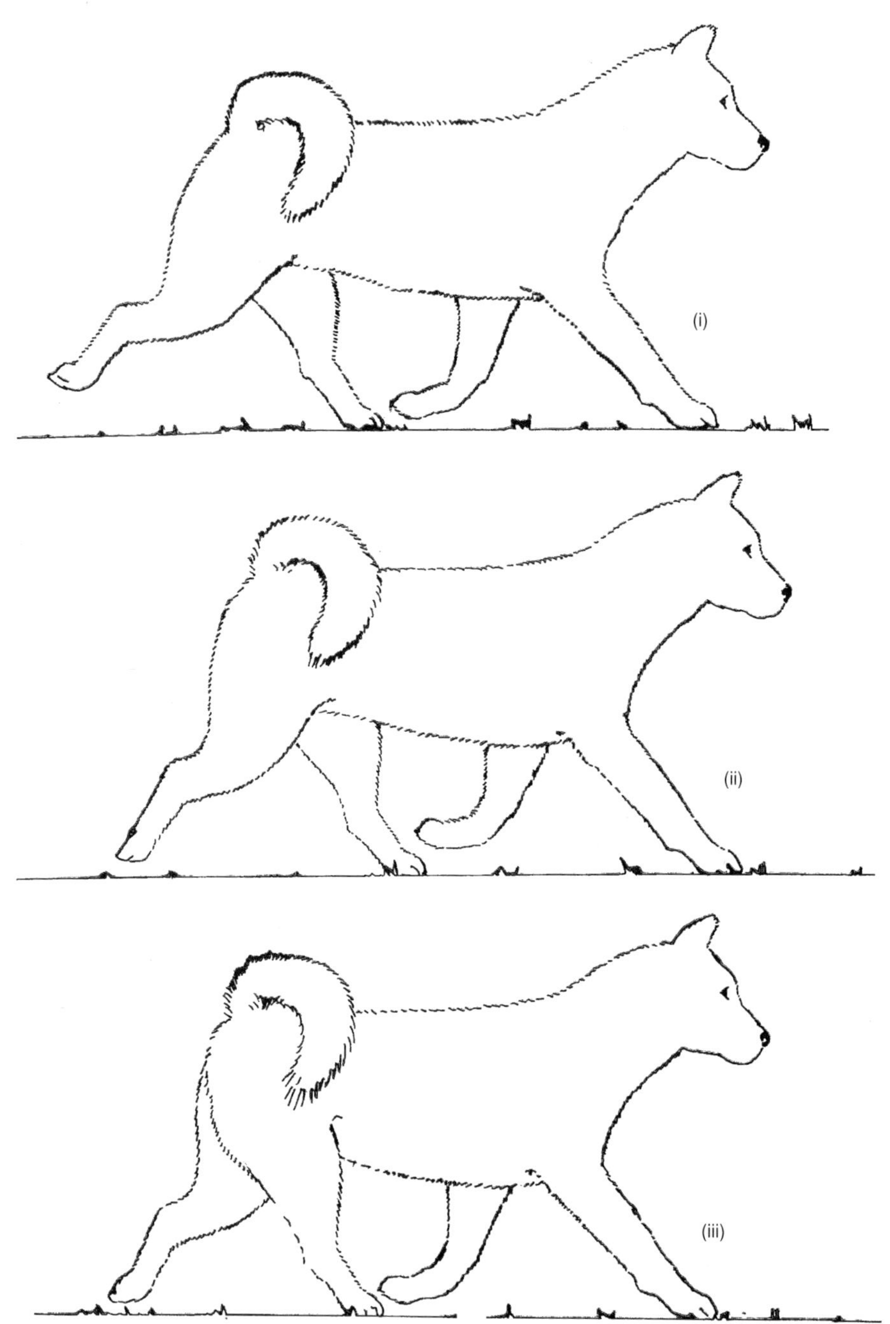

SIDE GAIT: (i).Incorrect. Extended reach in front, exaggerated 'kick' often confused with good movement. (ii) Correct. (iii). Incorrect. Pacing gait (ie both legs on same side of body move forward at the same time).

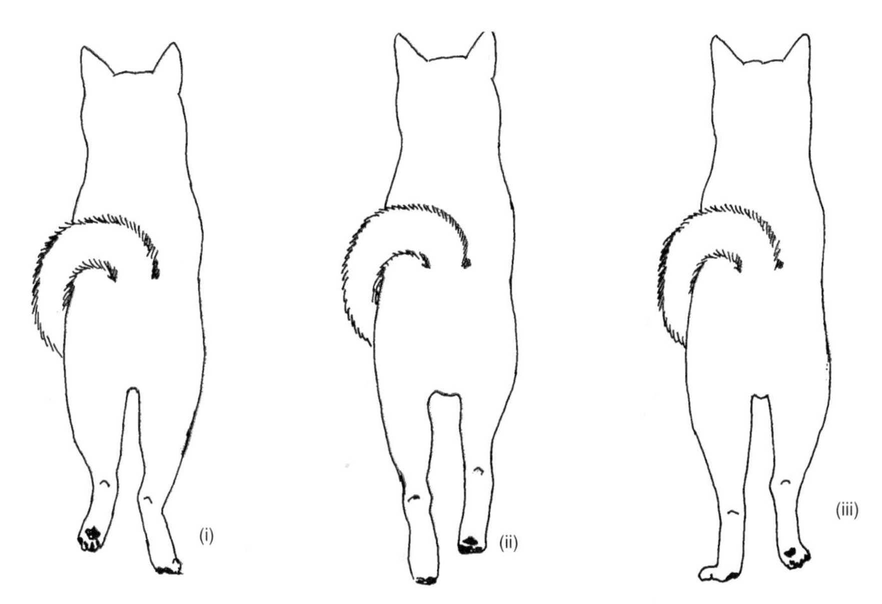

REAR MOVEMENT: (i) Cow hocked. (ii) Correct. (iii) Narrow rear. Feet turn out.

TEMPERAMENT

Dignified. One word says it all. The Akita should display his ancestry. He should be of proud bearing; not weak, or flighty and not cumbersome in his approach. He should appear courageous and out-going. He will almost certainly show dominance over other canines, if challenged. But he should never be aggressive to humans. In the exhibition ring, the dog's temperament should be judged just as his other characteristics are. Any unprovoked aggression should not be tolerated. It is not part of his breed standard and must be firmly penalised. Similarly, a dog which is shy and which backs off should be faulted. The Akita should always stand his ground firmly and accept all situations which come his way calmly.

SIZE

Size is important, although in the UK it does not carry any disqualification. Allowances would normally be made, but it is important to appreciate that the Akita is a big breed and one look at an undersized dog will tell you instantly that it does not look right. Similarly, an oversized dog will most certainly lose the ideal proportions which give the true Akita look and style. The smallest male can be 26 inches and the largest bitch can also be 26 inches, but the bitches should never be bigger than the dogs. Or if you prefer, the dogs should never be smaller than the bitches. Both males and females are solidly built and heavy. The smallest bitches weigh 70lbs or more, and the males can be as heavy as 120lbs.

CHAPTER FIVE

THE IMPORTANCE OF COLOUR

WE make no excuses for having a separate chapter on colour, for it is a subject which is constantly under discussion. We are not obsessed by it; our concern stems from the indisputable fact that if you disregarded colour, it would certainly disappear. Then we would not have an Akita, just an agouti-coloured dog, which, even if it had perfect proportions with soundness of mind and body, would still lack that special something which would make it an Akita. On numerous occasions we have asked people: 'What first attracted you to the Akita?' Ninety-nine times out of a hundred, the answer has been: "Because I saw a beautiful and striking dog." The response would hardly have been that if the dog had been the colour of the agouti rat.

The rich and varied colourings of the Akita are perhaps its greatest asset. Certainly they play a large part in the beauty and attractiveness of the animal. They are not a recent innovation. Japanese Akitas have always had pristine colours, similar to those which are found in all the Japanese arts. It is therefore not a modern whim that the Akita should be brilliant in colour but a definite requirement of the breed, and so it is included in the breed standard.

The breed standard states that any colour is acceptable. However, the statement is not as broad as it sounds, because the standard also states that the colours should be brilliant and clear. In other words, the colour should be a definite colour. When you look at a dog, you should not have to question its colour. You should know it is definitely red or black, silver or fawn. Pale, dilute colours are also wrong; rich and strong is the requirement of the standard. Solid whites can be either cream or ice-coloured, for there are two different shades of white in the Akita. The white in two-coloured dogs should be clear and not sparsed by other shadings or individual hairs, except that flecking, or 'ticking' as it is sometimes called, is permissible on the legs of two-coloured Akitas. There is no such thing as a tri-coloured Akita, nor are sable or salt-and-pepper acceptable. These colour descriptions are not acceptable to the standard. Silvers are silver, and not grey. One of our visitors, who was a car salesman in his business life, said that silver is like the metallic motor car, whereas grey is just grey — and that is quite a good way of describing it.

The colours which are most frequently used to describe the Akita are: black, white, fawn, red, silver, brown, silver-brindle, black-brindle and red-brindle. The colours which should not be used are: apricot, sable, tri-colour, parti, grey, yellow, gold, tawny, tan, spotted or roan. Many Akitas have a different coloured undercoat to the top coat. For example, a silver undercoat will have a black overlay of the coarse hairs. This is quite different to sable, where the one single hair has two colours on it. There is also the possibility of dilute colours, for instance when a colour such as silver is so pale as to be described as dilute. Dilute colourings seem to occur mostly in the red band and there are many Akitas which are orangey or beigey in appearance. This is quite different to fawn, which should always be the colour of a good quality camel coat.

Markings should be clearly defined. There should be no mingling of the colour with the white. Sometimes there will be a dark edge to the colour, separating it from the white. This is rather a strange phenomenon as it does rather belie the genetic possibilities of colourings in dogs. "Irish spotted" is a genetic term which describes a coloured dog with white socks, chest, collar and tail. It is interesting to note that the true Irish spotted markings only appear in certain breeding lines. The Japanese use the term "sesame" within their standard, but this is used nowhere else.

It is very wrong to breed or select animals just for their brilliant colours; there are many other factors that must be considered. But it is equally wrong to ignore colour for the sake of any other quality, be it soundness of movement, or structure or any other feature. There are often arguments, put forward by those who have dull, lack-lustre Akitas, claiming that the bright-coloured dogs are beautiful but either unsound or not as sound as their own dogs. This is quite a sweeping statement, considering that over the centuries hundreds of brightly-coloured Akitas have been champions. You will rarely hear the opposing argument, for most people who believe the Akita should be a brilliantly coloured dog also believe that absolute soundness is also part of the standard. The special point about colour is that it will almost certainly disappear, if it is not considered when breeding.

Basic soundness (perhaps with the exception of temperament) is in all canines. That is how they are made. Colouring and markings are, to some extent, fashioned by man and have subsequently become an essential part of the breed standard. Take, for instance, the Irish Setter. It would not be an Irish Setter and would certainly be penalised very heavily in the show ring, if it were not of the correct, true red colouring, proper to that breed. Colour really does have a very important part to play in the make-up of the Japanese Akita. It is a great factor in the beauty and distinctiveness of the breed. The clear, brilliant colours of the Akita are not found in any other breed, and discerning breeders and judges should always have regard for them, in order to preserve them for the future.

CHAPTER SIX

TEMPERAMENT

THE Akita is a big and powerful dog, with an interesting and complex temperament. It is important to understand your dog so that it is happy and enjoys the proper quality of life. The Japanese Akita is a lovable animal. It will adore its family, and it also enjoys the company of its own kind. Within its household, it will always choose one person that is extra special — and this is not necessarily the person that feeds the dog. Akitas rarely bark; they communicate with their eyes and through body language. You must learn to read their language and you will discover that your dog is wise and clever, fearless and steadfast. He is playful and will often instigate games. Many new owners accuse their Akita of being stubborn. However, after more experience they realise that it is merely determined.

If you need to chastise your dog, a sharp tap on the cheek or rump with a deep voiced "No", will bring it to a halt. If you have reared your dog correctly and taught it properly, it will respect you, and accept your wishes accordingly. Akitas have a terrific memory: fleeting meetings with people and other dogs are always remembered. Your dog will form habits easily, and it is up to you to see that they are good ones. It has a sixth sense about many things, and you should always heed it. If the dog barks at night or refuses to go into what he considers to be "bad ground", then take notice. The Akita rarely reacts for no reason. Although affectionate by nature, it does not like to be familiar with strangers. It prefers to remain aloof, saving its love for its immediate family and for regular visitors to the house. The Akita is a dog who wishes to live in peace. All it asks is for food, shelter, love and a happy and full life. He, as a dog, can only display his natural feelings. We as humans must analyse those feelings and partly mould them into an acceptable temperament for a domesticated dog.

No matter whatever anyone may try to tell you, temperament is an inherited quality. It can be moulded, but never altered. Whatever the temperament of the parents, and perhaps the grandparents, the children will have either some, or all of the inherited traits. This is one of the many reasons why you should check out the parents of your Akita before you buy it. Once a puppy is born, the die is cast. It is then up to you to ensure that the in-born good traits are brought to the fore and any bad traits, are moulded into acceptable behaviour.

RESPECT

This is by far the most important aspect of temperament, as it forms the basis of your relationship with your dog. The Akita is naturally dominant. It cannot help having this trait and so you must accept it. That does not mean to say that it will attack or attempt to exert its authority over every human or dog that it meets. Quite the contrary. Dominance is only shown in the true Akita when it is necessary. If it is challenged, by the eye, stance or growl of any other dog, your Akita will instantly stand its ground and, if necessary, move in and sort out the challenger. It will rarely start the fight, except when it is protecting its family, or their property. It may also make a stand against another human if it feels the situation is a definite threat to its owner and family. In this case you could argue that the Akita is being protective, rather than domineering; but in either case, it feels the need to be master of the situation.

You will never remove this trait, and so you must teach your Akita to respect your wishes. If you have a caller at the door, the Akita is instantly on guard. It will not throw itself at the door, barking loudly. If it has grown up with you and respects you, it will just watch and wait by your side, watching for your signals. If you say "Okay, this is a friend," then your friend should be allowed to come into the house. If, however, you are apprehensive about the caller, your words and attitude will tell your Akita to be watchful. But it must understand that it has to wait for a signal before it "moves in". If you do not "read" your Akita and so fail to understand it, you will have no control. You must respect its natural instincts, but you must be able to command its respect. For this is the key to a co-operative and amenable dog. It will respond because it respects you, never because it fears you or is subservient to you.

DOMINANCE

This is a part of the breed and it can never be changed. It is a dangerous asset and is made worse because the Akita rarely displays its intentions to anyone. It can be on its lead, standing quite happily, wagging its tail, and not appearing to be taking any interest in the dogs that are present. But you must not be complacent. You will not always see or sense the messages being sent out by these dogs to each other. In less than an instant, your Akita can pull free from your grasp. It is a strong and fast animal. When you are out and about with an Akita, you must always be fully aware of your surroundings and of any dogs in the vicinity, particularly those that are within the powerful leap-range of your dog.

Dominance is a natural trait and is present from a very early age. If you already own another dog, you must accept that your Akita will not allow itself to be dominated or challenged by it. When people ask if their Akita will live with their Jack Russell Terrier, the answer is; it depends on the temperament of the Jack Russell. If the terrier is passive in character, then it will never challenge the Akita and so the Akita will never have to exert its dominance. If, on the other hand, the terrier is dominant and tries to tell the Akita that it is the boss, then you will have difficulty in keeping them both happy.

Take the case of a four month old Akita bitch, called Lulu. She was purchased by some very nice people, who owned another dog of the Spitz breed. They went away happy and fully understanding both the dominant trait of the Akita and being already aware of the natural independence which is in all Spitz breeds. Lulu settled down, happily living in their house, and care was always taken to ensure that the male Spitz, who was top dog in their kennel, was not allowed to meet Lulu. Of course, the inevitable happened. A visitor failed to close the back door properly, and the male Spitz came bounding into the house. Lulu was underneath the kitchen table. The Spitz ran towards her, and Lulu did not flinch, for Akitas always stand their ground. She set her eye on the approaching, dominant Spitz and just looked at him. Spitz breeds often see things quicker than other breeds, and the male stopped in his tracks and looked at Lulu. As far as he was concerned, she was on his territory, but Lulu, who was only four-months-old, stared at the Spitz and sent out the message "don't even think about it. I am an Akita, and I am the dominant one." The Spitz male turned and walked away.

The owner had dashed into the kitchen when she had heard the door open and had stood rooted to the spot, fearing the worst. She had seen her male Spitz in action before, and she was astounded there was no blood shed. The power of the Akita's eye had told the Spitz not to come forward. This was not an exceptional occurrence, the power of the Akita is such that most dogs will get the message.

POSSESSION

This is closely tied in with dominance — and as far as the Akita is concerned, there are no half measures. Let's take food. You are the food-giver, and you are loved for it. But once you have put that bowl of food down, it does not belong to you anymore, and only a fool would try to take it away. Your Akita might be wagging its tail, but it will not let you take away something that it now regards as its own.

An Akita owner once professed that the way to train an Akita to respect you and to behave as you wished, was to prepare its food, and then just as the dog thinks you are putting the dish down, take it away. Now we call that both stupid and extremely unkind. Just think of how the Akita will interpret the situation. Here it is hungry — waiting for its meal. Then just as it is about to tuck in, the meal disappears. The Akita is bound to feel puzzled and resentful. After all, it has done nothing wrong. You have to keep faith with your Akita; you should not bully it or tease it. If you are feeding the dog, you must feed it. Then it will appreciate what you are doing, rather than wishing someone else would provide for it.

Possession seems to be territorial, and not just a matter of macho dominance. The Akita will naturally protect its family and its territory. It might greet your visitors with hugs and kisses when it is out in the garden, but when it is in its kennel or back in the house, it will start guarding. It is also possessive of its possessions — its blanket or its water bowl.

Take the case of two young bitches that were taken to a dog show. Suzie was given a drink by her owner, and Emma wanted to share. Both bitches were seven months old, very happy and good tempered. The full bowl of water is put down for Suzie. Emma moves in and Suzie gives her a look: "Okay, you can share. " So they both drink until they get down to the last drop. Suzie and Emma both look up from the bowl. Now remember, it is Suzie's water and Emma is the guest, or put a better way, the intruder. The bitches stand still, no one moves. The owners are remarking on how friendly the two girls are, but the experienced eye can see a potential hazard. And yes, there it is: suddenly the two bitches fly at each other, and a brief but keen skirmish ensues, with Emma coming off worst.

Now to analyse. You would have thought that Emma, as the intruder would have been determined to come out on top. But no, Suzie had the water and she had allowed Emma to drink. But the last drop was hers, and her natural instinct to defend her possession became dominant as Emma pushed her luck a little too far. Fortunately, both owners acted quickly, and no real harm was done. Then the two bitches sat happily, side by side, for the rest of the day. As far as they were concerned, the matter was settled. Akitas do not have a natural desire to fight, but they will obey their instincts. In most cases, these fundamental traits of character are related to the need to survive and they should not be interfered with.

ADAPTABILITY

The Akita should adapt to any situation, whether you ask for a guard, a watchdog, a show dog, or just a companion; the Akita will fit the bill. You can never physically control this powerful animal; you must develop an understanding of its mind. We often hear from owners, who are struggling to control their dogs. When we actually see one of these dogs, we find, more often than not, that the Akita is behaving normally, but the owner is in trouble. He is not on the same wavelength as his dog. When we discuss the problem and demonstrate what we mean, we usually hear, within a short space of time that all is well. Take the case of Fido, a young Akita male, just six months old, purchased as a show dog, and to be handled by the lady owner.

Unfortunately, this Akita decided that the man of the family was to be his " special person". The lady demonstrated the Akita's unwillingness either to show himself off in stance or to move smartly around the show ring. He just wanted to return to the husband for a cuddle. Experience is everything in these matters, and we could see at once that this was not a happy dog. Why did he wish to return to the husband? The lady loved him; but we could see that she loved him so much that she did not want to force her wishes on the dog. "I don't want to upset him," she said. "Rubbish!" we said. "The puppy has a keen brain, he wants to learn. You are just trying, half-heartedly, to make him work for you. He likes being cuddled and praised, he does not understand the extra joy of being praised in return for a job well done." We took the dog and led him on to the lawn. We made him stand. We made him trot. We tapped his cheek and rump to exert a little authority. He did not want to do it, but he did. He kept looking back at the husband, but with plenty of encouragement he carried on. He realised it was better to move of his own accord than to be pulled along by the lead. As soon as he did something correctly, he got plenty of praise — and then on with the lesson. Within twenty minutes the puppy was trotting around. "This is not so bad," he thought. "If I do it right, I get a bigger cuddle." When the lady had a go, the dog continued to do as it was told. It had come to the realisation that it was fun to do something right and to be praised for it. A few days later the owners telephoned us to report that every time the lady approached Fido with the show lead, he went mad with excitement. They now had a real Akita.

Akitas as a breed will learn as much as you are prepared to teach. Some may need a little convincing, but once you have overcome their initial reluctance, the dog, stimulated by new challenges, will enjoy a better quality of life. The Akita has a complex temperament, ranging from powerful and "aggressive" determination to gentle and absolute dedication. When the dog is understood by its owner, it will make a superb companion. It offers a degree of sensitivity that is unsurpassed by any other breed. As Akita owners always say "having owned an Akita, I shall never own anything else but an Akita".

CHAPTER SEVEN

OWNING AN AKITA

SO you wish to own a Japanese Akita? A good decision, or at least we hope that it will prove to be so. There is no doubt that the breed is lovely to look at, and this is generally what attracts would-be owners in the first instance. It is, however, not so simple, for here we have a large, very powerful dog. It has a mind of its own, to a certain degree, and it will probably live to be about twelve years old and so you need to make a long-term commitment. The average Akita will adore its family, but it will be aloof with strangers, so it is not always an easy dog. It has to be accommodated, cared for and respected. It will fit into any lifestyle, but it does demand, and deserve, attention.

If you are planning to buy an Akita, you should ask yourself: "Why do I want a dog of this breed?" The reason itself is unimportant, but you must ensure that the qualities inherent in an Akita, comply with your lifestyle. For instance, you may want your Akita to live with your three male toy poodles, so you must establish whether or not this would be a feasible proposition. You may want your Akita to live outside, alone. In that case, you should be honest with the breeder, and ask if your Akita would be happy in that situation. And so on. Equally, if you are a breeder and wish to sell your puppies, you should be truthful about the breed to the would-be purchaser and tell them whether the Akita would live peacefully with the toy poodles or whether it would accept living outside, on its own. Whichever category you are in, it is vital for the future well-being of the Akita to give careful thought to either the sale, or the purchase of a puppy.

DOG OR BITCH?

What do we see in the male? There is no doubt that the male of the Akita breed is the most striking and majestic. He displays the characteristic strength and power, and he can look and act the most regal and proud. He has the strong bone and substance, which is so attractive, and he will have an impressive head. He looks formidable, almost frightening, fulfilling all the qualities which the breed standard demands. There is no disputing that he is the epitome of the breed.

Pretty, stylish, graceful, yet still powerful. These are the qualities that are admired in the female Akita. She may not be so big and fine as the male, but she has style and beauty, and strength of character too. And she is the one who holds the key to the future, for she is capable of producing one of those fine, majestic males. The old saying: " A good bitch is worth her weight in gold" is one hundred per cent right. You can always pay the stud fee for whichever dog you consider to be the best in the world, but you would be unlikely to be able to buy the best bitch. So not only is your chosen bitch beautiful, typical and full of character. She is priceless. She is so often underestimated, so often outshone by the males. But look a little deeper and you will realise that she holds that precious key.

All too often judges will penalise a bitch in the show ring for looking mature or showing "frills" — a slight showing of the teats and mammary area under the belly. But why? How can she perpetuate the species if she does not whelp and feed her puppies? We must accept that she has a role to play as mother. The sire can do his bit and within an hour or so he has made a complete recovery and is free from his duty. But the bitch faces a far greater task. We should admire the males for their magnificent physical appearance, but the bitches have a different, deeper beauty which should be recognised and equally admired.

So you come to the choosing. In truth, the temperament of all Akitas is the same — dog or bitch will display the same traits. Both will love their family. The males are certainly stronger and they tend to go through an adolescence which is not an easy time. The bitches are less strong, a little less imposing and perhaps a little more amenable. It is not an easy choice and it should be made carefully.

CHOOSING A BREEDER

Once you have decided to become an owner you should make a thorough investigation of the breed. You should visit as many kennels as possible, and if you wish, it is a good idea to travel to the shows, which are the breeders' shop window. You will eventually decide which Akitas you like, and which you feel represent the standard. You should then check out the pedigrees of these dogs to see if they all come from the same breeding and to establish whether they are "common" to the breeder of your choice. This means that there are a number of this type and it is not a one-off. If it is common, you should be able to buy your ideal Akita from a selection of breeders that are using similar bloodlines. It is no good looking at just one dog and saying: "That's my ideal, but I don't like anything else from that kennel." The chances are that when you buy your puppy, it will look like the majority of the kennel's produce, and it will not resemble the one dog you liked. If, on the other hand, you find a breeder or breeders who continually produce similar-looking dogs, you can be almost sure that the Akita puppy you buy will grow up to be of the same type.

The next step is to visit the breeder. Ask to see photos of other dogs they have bred. Check their dogs' ancestors. Ask questions with regard to hereditary problems and growth patterns. Check out the breeder's attitude towards his dogs and the cleanliness of the kennels. Check the temperament and attitude of their dogs. Are they happy, well-fed and full of vitality? Or are they hiding somewhere in a corner, down at the bottom of a run of kennels, forgotten save for those short times when they produce puppies? Make sure you insist on meeting some of the dogs face to face. If you are going to live with one of this breed, you need to meet it on home ground. Show rings are fine for showing off the physical attributes, but the atmosphere is false and the dogs know that they are there on display and have to behave. You need to see an Akita playing in the garden, running round the kitchen, sitting at your feet. You need to see the dog in normal, everyday circumstances. When you are happy with everything, book your puppy and wait. Beware of the breeder who says:"You can take the puppy today, if you want." Generally speaking, good stock has to be ordered in advance.

You should also expect the bona fide breeder to ask you many questions about yourself. They will be anxious to ensure that one of their precious dogs is going to a suitable home. If you are a new breeder, there are a few tips to bear in mind which will help you to assess the prospective owners. Watch they way they react to your dogs. Do they obviously relate to them, or are they more worried about getting dog-hairs on their clothes? To observe this all-important reaction, it is a good idea to show off at least one Akita which is shedding its coat. Do they ask questions? They should ask lots of them. Try and find out about the type of accommodation, both house and garden. And ask about the working hours of the owners. Do they have any other animals? Do they have lots of free time to give to the dog? Have they owned a dog before? Do they realise they will have this puppy when it is old and, perhaps, frail, needing extra care. You should never feel shy about asking all these questions, whether you are a breeder or a would-be owner. A conversation over a cup of tea can tell both parties a lot and could save a lot of heartache. After all, the Akita cannot speak for itself; we have to make sure of its future.

CHOOSING A PUPPY

A litter of chunky six-week-old puppies that look like little teddy bears will capture the heart of anyone. Akita puppies are very beautiful and appealing, but, in the main, they do not reflect the adult dog. If they have been reared well they will look absolutely marvellous and will be irresistible. But hold on, slow down! Remember, everything is genetic. The qualities and faults of both of the parents will come out in these puppies. These things may not be apparent at this stage, but they are there, and will emerge as the dog matures. Our advice is to always insist on seeing both parents of a litter before you buy. This is an absolute must and should never be denied to you. Your puppy will look like mum or dad, or both. It will have characteristics of its grandmother or grandfather, or a combination of all these influences. It will not look like the beautiful Akita you saw at the show, which was bred by a completely different breeder. The dogs you are viewing at the kennels represent the type your Akita will grow into. Is that what you want? If it is, great! Go ahead and enjoy yourselves. Spend hours, if the breeder will let you, looking at the dogs and playing with their puppies. All genuine breeders will be only too happy to spare you their time. At our kennels we have endless streams of visitors. People say: "Don't you get bored?" But we never do when we are discussing the future well-being of our Akitas.

When you are trying to choose, look carefully at the puppies and try to work out their individual traits and characters. See how they conduct themselves. Check out their markings, if they have any. Does the pup have a scissor bite, even though it still has its milk teeth? Look at the shape of the head, the set of tail, the shoulder-lay, and the rear strength. Many characteristics are apparent, even at this young age. Any breeder, worth his salt, will tell you the differences between his puppies.

It is only a fool that allows himself to be landed with a puppy that has simply been allocated to him. You have the right to look and to choose. Of course, you have to accept that there may have been others who had a choice before you, but do not worry. If the breeder is genuine, he or she is not going to let you go away with any puppy which is not, to some extent, your choosing. Similarly, many people have an ideal dog in mind, and then, when they see the litter, they fall for a completely different sort of pup. Fine! We always look at the puppies and look at the people and then try to match the two. Generally would-be purchasers select different puppies and it all works out. Do not ever feel obliged to take a puppy, just because you have booked one. If you don't particularly like what you see, ask to wait until another litter is born. Again, any genuine breeder will not mind at all. As long as you are not wasting his time, he will be happy to see you later on. In any event, there is probably someone else waiting on the sidelines, hoping that you back out so that he can come in!

When you have chosen your puppy, ask questions about its general health, toilet habits, food intake and worming status. You should check that it is Kennel Club registered, if it is supposed to be. If you wish to have a receipt for your payment, remember to ask for one then. If the registration certificate is not to hand, ask for a written promise of one. If both sides are genuine, these arrangements should pose no problems. It is sad, but the days of a gentleman's handshake are long gone and it is better to be safe than sorry. Some breeders will have their puppies checked over by a vet the day before they are due to leave. This would only be a general check and does not guarantee the breed characteristics of the puppy, or protect you from any future problems, hereditary or otherwise. It does, however, tell you that the puppy is physically in good shape. There is no reason why you should not take your newly acquired puppy to your own vet when you get it home. A similar check will tell you that all is well; or, if there are any problems, you can immediately go back to the breeder and — more important — attend to the health of the puppy. Responsible ownership of a Japanese Akita begins right at the beginning. As they say: "Today is the first day of the rest of my life."

CHAPTER EIGHT

CARE OF THE AKITA

THE day-to-day care of your Akita will have a great bearing on its physical and mental well-being. You should provide a comfortable place to sleep, free from wet and draughts, a constant supply of clean water in a clean bowl (Akitas drink enormous amounts), regular, nutritious meals, some grooming and exercise, and lots of attention and love.

FEEDING

Akitas do well on many kinds of food and so their diet can be a matter of individual choice. However, the Akita is a large dog and so a regular intake of all vitamins, plus calcium is essential. Two meals per day are preferable as the dog is deep-bodied and also drinks a lot of water. One large meal will swell the gut, whereas two smaller meals will help to reduce the risk of torsion or bloat. Your Akita will also benefit greatly from this added attention. A well-balanced diet is infinitely better than a skimpy meal, plus additives. Adult Akitas do not eat as much food as you would think, but growing puppies eat far more than you could ever imagine.

EXERCISE

Akitas enjoy exercise, they love to run and play. They like to play football and other games, and love to hunt in the hedgerows when they are out in the country. Youngsters, in particular, need adequate exercise. It has been proved that young, growing dogs need exercise to develop their muscles. The Akita is very heavy and grows rapidly: strong muscles are needed to give support to the growing bones. Once the dog is fully grown, moderate exercise is sufficient. You do not need to walk for miles and miles as you have to with some breeds. A large garden, in some cases, would be enough. But Akitas love to go out and about, and it would be a shame to deprive them. There are many theories on how the amount of exercise can change the eventual gait of the Akita. In our experience the style of gait is purely structural. You can rear and exercise every Akita in the same manner and end up with completely different styles of gait. You can, however, cause damage to ligaments and bones by incorrect exercise. It is a fine line to draw and is a matter which should be discussed in depth with the breeder of your puppy.

HOUSING

Akitas enjoy comfort, and bedding in the form of blankets and cushions will generally be much appreciated — but in their own way. If you make a nice, neat bed for an Akita, it will only be a matter of minutes before it has rummaged the blankets into a ball. They may tear the bedding to shreds, but they will rarely swallow the pieces. All dogs are different, and there are those who might prefer no bedding at all. You should provide whatever they require. If it is being kept in the house, your Akita will select its own resting place, and wherever possible, you should accede to its request. If you are keeping the dog outside, it may prefer the security and cosiness of a closed kennel door at night, or it might like to stay outside, without restrictions. Again, let the dog choose.

The Akita is heavily-built and so it is likely to develop a pressure point from lying in one position. That is to say that the hair, usually on an elbow or hock joint, will be worn off simply because the dog lies in a particular position and places the greatest weight on that section of its body. These pressure points, if not attended to, will become callouses and the hair will appear stained. These places need regular care and attention, not only for the sake of appearance, but more importantly for the welfare and comfort of the dog. The well-known and easily available E45 cream is an excellent preparation which, if applied regularly, will keep any problem at bay.

GROOMING

A good brush and a good rounded-toothed metal comb are all the tools you need to keep your Akita in top-class condition. Akitas' coats do not cause much trouble, there is no doggy odour and there should be no hair loss at all, except at the regular moult. There is no real need to groom every day: three times a week will keep your Akita looking beautiful, and what a difference a five-minute brush makes. Akitas enjoy this attention and accept the procedure willingly.

Legs, feet and underarms should be washed regularly to keep your Akita sweet-smelling and looking clean. Check ears regularly, although problems are not common, and keep an eye on the pads and the base of the tail. Always be on the look-out for those unfriendly little nasties, the fleas and ticks of this world. Teeth should be checked and cleaned regularly from puppyhood. However, the teeth of many Akitas discolour at a very early age. To date, no one knows why this should happen.

THE COAT

The Akita will fully cast its coat once a year, normally on a regular cycle. However, changes in climate and sometimes re-housing can affect the coat-change cycle. The worst cast will be the first. When your Akita casts its first coat — and this can be any time from seven months to eighteen months — it can be quite a traumatic experience for you and your dog. The whole coat will go, all the undercoat and some of the top coat. The tail will resemble a rat's and even ears will look thin and bedraggled. The tendency is to worry that your dog is ill, or that you are giving him the wrong diet. Gone is that lovely and beautiful dog! Instead you have a walking skeleton, virtually hairless, muscle tone has vanished, the legs look thin with no flesh on them, the cheeks have disappeared, the pasterns are loose, and the feet are flatter than usual. Don't panic! It is perfectly normal for your Akita to suffer a complete loss of condition at this time.

It is important that you keep feeding at a good level. Do not use supplements; it is not necessary. Just feed the dog its normal diet, perhaps in a slightly larger quantity. Once the coat is out, nothing will happen for a couple of weeks. Then, one day, you will see a glimmer of new bloom. Full recovery occurs in the twinkling of an eye. Well, perhaps that is a slight exaggeration, but the return to full coat is remarkably fast, and soon your beautiful puppy is restored to you. The dog will not notice this change at all; it will be just as happy and active during the moult as before. You will be the one who feels bad about it all!

At any coat-cast, it is mainly the undercoat which is shed. This will come off rather like a fleece. The best remedy is to bath once the coat is loose, and then groom out the old hair. You can spin the hair, if you like, and then knit it into a pullover — it is incredibly warm. Bitches tend to cast more than males but the time of the coat-cast does not follow the same pattern as their season. Some Akitas may go off their food when they are moulting, but appetite will invariably be restored once the new coat growth appears. Once the new hair begins to come through, regular grooming will aid the formation of that lovely plushy appearance. Quality of coat is a matter of genetics. You cannot make a poor coat better, but you can ensure a good coat looks its best by feeding the correct diet and by regular grooming.

TRANSPORT

Most Akitas are good travellers. You will find they love to jump into any open car-door. Do take care though, for remember that they are a very heavy breed and are naturally inquisitive. They may well stand while they are travelling and there is always the danger of them falling over if you have to brake suddenly. We always prefer to crate our travelling dogs, or at least restrict their travelling area to avoid the danger of them being thrown around.

OVER-BREEDING

It may be tempting for some people to breed with a good bitch, every time she comes in season — but this should be resisted for a number of reasons. Firstly, the chances are that she will start to produce poor-quality puppies. More importantly, having too many litters would impose undue physical and mental stress on the bitch. Please do not place your bitch into this situation, she deserves better. She should be bred from if she has something to offer the breed, but she should never be used solely as a producer of puppies.

TRAINING

The basic rule for training is a simple one. Train with love, patience and gentleness, but with firmness and a dominant attitude. Your Akita will naturally have a strong affection for you and will want to please. You should play the part of leader, and a bit of bribery will not come amiss.

The best way to chastise an Akita is to face the dog full-on, and using the flat of your hand, tap him on the cheek. The fact that you have confronted the dog in this manner will make it understand instantly that you mean something, and its natural curiosity makes it want to find out what it is. You must then explain that you will not tolerate its bad behaviour. The second time you do this, the dog will react in the same non-plussed manner. But as you approach the dog on the third occasion, with an outstretched hand and with that look in your eye, it will realise that you mean business and it will succumb. Do beware though, because you are likely to get leaped on and licked to death! Don't ignore this response. It is the Akita's way of saying: "I love you and I do accept your wishes." The bond of friendship and trust which can be formed from training your dog is one of the most rewarding aspects of owning an Akita. Advice on training for the specialist fields of obedience, agility and rescue should be sought from those who are proficient in these activities. There are Akita owners who are active in all these areas, and they are more than willing to help anyone with a specialist interest.

CHAPTER NINE

BREEDING

BREEDING any animal is a serious business and should be taken seriously by the humans who instigate the life cycle. We are all custodians of the Akita and the breed's future is in our hands, and our hands alone. We have a responsibility to breed Akitas which are true to type, with the distinctive characteristics, both physical and temperamental, of their race. There is no place for individual whims and fancies. Only the Akita's natural designs must be considered.

TO BREED OR NOT TO BREED?

Those new to the Akita breed will eventually ask three questions: "Should I get involved in the breeding these dogs?" " Should I let my bitch have a litter?" and the more unusual one, "Should I allow my male to be a sire?" Those with more experience would ask the more apposite question: "Is my Akita worthy of becoming a parent and passing on its own, and its ancestors' virtues and faults to future generations?"

In the natural world, animals select their own mates. This process ensures that only those fit enough, and carrying the vital characteristics of their particular species, perfectly adapted for survival, will produce the future generation. In the world of the domesticated dog, it is you, the owner and temporary custodian of the breed, who is one hundred per cent responsible for the decisions. You will decide upon the parents, and so you will decide upon the future members of the breed. You cannot blame those who bred the animals before you, those who produced your own dog or bitch or their parents. They may have been wrong or right, but that was their decision. This time the decision is yours. The responsibility is tremendous: you must accept it and act on it.

You should never decide to get involved in breeding for any reason, other than a total regard for the puppies you will be bringing into the world. It is not good enough to plan a litter, hoping the pups will turn out to be better-looking than their mother or more true to type than their father. If you are deeply interested in Akitas, you will have read and understood the standard for the breed. This is the standard which ALL Akitas must conform to. They are certainly not going to be clones, but they must adhere closely to their stated descriptions. The saying: "You can't make a silk purse out of a sow's ear" is absolutely true in this case. There is always the odd "flier", when two animals of mediocre or poor quality produce an exceptionally fine specimen. But this is rare indeed, and is not worth the risk. And what about the flier's littermates? You must be super-critical of your Akita and it must be of exceptional quality to be selected for producing future generations. It is sometimes hard to accept that the lovely Akita, which is your pride and joy, has proven hereditary problems. These may not always be visual, and you may feel that other people are breeding from Akitas which are inferior to your dog. But you must be resolute, for your own peace of mind and for the future of the breed.

PLANNING A LITTER

Once you have taken the decision to breed with your Akita, you must investigate the skeletons in the cupboard. You must find out about its ancestors from the breeders, and discover the dominant characteristics that are being carried in your Akita's genes. These may not be be visually apparent or known to you. You must not allow yourself to be fobbed off with lies or half-truths. Nor by explanations like "Well, that was the only thing wrong, so we risked it." There is a simple truth in to bear in mind when breeding animals, and that is: "Like produces like." This applies equally to visual and non-visual characteristics and traits. There is no doubt that every Akita produced will show some trait of either, or both, of its parents, and that should be the basis on which you make your decision.

Although caution is a by-word in breeding, it would be ludicrous to suggest only perfect dogs and bitches should be bred from. Of course, no dog is perfect, but there are many which do not reach the desired standard. If your dog falls into that category you should be brave enough to admit it and say: "Okay, I love my dog as a pet, but I will find another Akita to purchase and use for breeding." That would be totally responsible, and realistic and you would be admired for making that decision.

When you are confident that your Akita is suitable to use for breeding, the next consideration is the welfare of the bitch and the future puppies. No matter how good in quality your Akita may be, you must not breed or get involved with breeding if this could cause pain or hardship to either the parent, or the resultant puppies. Remember, it is you who will be blamed for producing puppies with physical defects. It is you who will be responsible if the dam suffers pain and distress during the pregnancy, the birth, or the post natal nursing time. The owner of the sire is also caught up in this web of responsibility. All too often we hear of puppies, sired by one of the top dogs in the breed, being sold in pet shops or puppy farms by people who have no knowledge of the breed they are selling. To say: "I only allowed them to use my dog," is totally unacceptable. The breeder who decides to use a dog at stud carries as great a burden as the breeder who uses a bitch to breed from. Both are responsible for the future of the breed.

The owner of a stud dog can face a very difficult dilemma. Suppose you have a superb male, which is a proven sire of quality puppies, and an owner comes along with a sub-standard bitch that he wants to breed from. What do you do? A look at the bitch tells you that she is not really good enough — she did not carry off any honours in the show ring when she was being assessed against the breed standard. Do you try to persuade the bitch's owner to think again and not use the bitch for breeding? Do you agree to the mating and collect the stud fee, hoping your dog will counter-balance the bitch's poor qualities? Or do you refuse to allow the mating, and send the owner on his way? It is a very difficult decision to make. It is made easier if the bitch's owner appears to see the future offspring as pound notes. You can then turn down owner and bitch, and hope that other stud dog owners will do the same.

It is far more difficult to try to convince the owner that his bitch is unsuitable for breeding, for he is certain to challenge your authority. There is merit in discussion, and perhaps the outcome will be favourable at least for the breed, though not for you, as you will have talked yourself out of the stud fee. Sometimes it is obvious that the owner is absolutely determined to use his bitch, no matter what. This is surely the ultimate dilemma. If you send the bitch and owner on their way, you are left with the dubious satisfaction of saying "I told you so" when the offspring appear. Or do you decide that, as the bitch's owner is so determined to have a litter, it would make more sense for your dog to be the sire. He has proved himself as a sire of good puppies, and so in normal expectancy terms, half the puppies should be of better quality than the dam.

Unfortunately, there is no simple answer. It is easier to be high-minded when you have just started in the breed and to say: "Oh no! I would never let my male mate a bitch like that," without really thinking, for all things appear black and white. In truth, there are many shades of grey, and individual cases should be judged on their merit. It is not our intention to try to persuade you either to get involved in breeding or not. That is your decision. All we ask is that you weigh up your decision very carefully. We have learned over the years that there are many heartbreaks; there are the dogs you would love to use for breeding, but physically they would not stand up to it, there is the ideal dog or bitch, which proves to be infertile. And there are the joys of taking the gamble, for it is a gamble every time in some sense, and producing lovely puppies which grow into happy and healthy adults, true representatives of their breed.

GENETIC SELECTION

If the Akita was selecting its own mate in the wild, it would pay heed to the fitness of associate companions, their power and forcefulness and their scent, indicating the right time for mating. These factors would bring about a stability of virtues because of the close proximity of partners, and the most likely mate would be the strongest and fittest. It would also lead to any faults becoming dominant thereby naturally selecting poorer animals which would not survive so well and would probably not breed on. This was how the Akita developed and and hence produced the distinctive breed which we now enjoy as a domestic dog.

Obviously there are some characteristics and traits which have been introduced by man through specialised breeding programmes, but the Akita, as opposed to perhaps the Bulldog, is a natural breed. It evolved through natural selection before it was recognised by man. In the domestic situation, it is now man that takes on the role of choosing suitable mates. We also have modern medicine and surgery available to us, which means that some animals are used for breeding, which might not have survived in the wild. We select the mate and therefore we dictate the joining of the genes which, in their millions, form the future offspring.We should always take a conscientious look at the virtues and faults of both parents, and try to work out the likely result of that particular mating. However, nature can still surprise us and the result can be better — or worse— than we expected.

There are many schools of thought on whether to line-breed, whether to out-cross, or to in-breed. Decisions about culling and restrictions on future breeding are also the subject of much discussion. Each decision is a personal one, but we should always remember that the Akita is a naturally beautiful animal, distinctive from any other breed, and it should be preserved as such. He must also be fit and sound in mind and body.

HEREDITARY

Every single characteristic is inherited through genes, be it visual characteristics, the method of bodily functions, or behavioural traits. If you look at the parents, you should get a good idea of what the puppies will be like, though each puppy will be different due to the endless permutations of the individual genes. There are however, certain dominant basic characteristics which will always reproduce themselves. For instance, the formation of the mouth will produce a similar formation of a mouth. And so the selection of any mate will tell you that your resultant puppies will bear the characteristics of their parents, grandparents, or great-grandparents and so on.

It is generally accepted that the first three generations are the most influential, if you go further back there will only be the odd trait which will appear dominant. These first three generations should form your future. They should be carefully investigated and studied. You should take the trouble to see these animals and their relatives, wherever possible. For example, try and see the nephews and nieces of your intended pair, the half-brothers and sisters of your future puppies. Visual assessment and actual contact is the only real way to ensure that you fully understand what you are about to produce. Names on a pedigree, even if they are champions are meaningless, unless you know the animals themselves, or have sound evidence of their characteristics and character. You must never leave anything to chance. Remember all things are genetic, and like will produce like.

CHOOSING THE MATE

This is mostly a matter for the owner of the bitch, who will be selecting a stud dog. However, the owner of the selected sire has an absolute right to know the good and bad things about the bitch that is brought to his male, for his dog will be responsible for half the puppies' inherited qualities. When you are planning to breed from a bitch, look at her closely and assess her qualities; in which areas does she excel, what are her failings? Does she have any problem which you would not want to reproduce? You should then take your investigation a stage further; where do her good points come from?

When all this has been considered, you can choose the mate. First of all, work out what are you aiming for? Do you wish to produce Akitas which look like the dam? Or do you wish to produce Akitas which look like your chosen sire? Do you wish to combine the two and produce something of your own? This is all a matter of personal choice, but the important thing is to have a definite plan in mind. Otherwise all you are doing is producing dogs called Akitas, but you will have done nothing to benefit the future of the breed. Let us consider using examples; suppose your bitch excels in ear type and carriage, you must select a mate who also has good ears and carriage, and that should ensure that you will not loose the quality. If you choose a mate which has poor ears and carriage, in theory only half of your puppies will have the correct ears and carriage, but of course, it is not that simple. If your bitch fails in tail set, perhaps being low and loose, and you choose a mate with similar tail and set, the chances are that you will "stamp in" that particular undesirable trait. Therefore, you should choose a mate with the correct tail and set, and hope that half of your puppies will carry the mate's introduced qualities. If you have looked at other relatives, you may discover that your bitch was perhaps the only one in her litter with this problem, so it is not so important as if all of her litter had carried the same problem.

Basically you must choose a mate which compliments your bitch. The most common mistake that people make is thinking that a large over-sized bitch is going to produce nice middle-sized puppies if she is mated to a small male. In fact she will produce some big puppies and some small puppies, because neither parent carries the gene for middle-sized puppies. What you should do is mate your bitch to the correct-sized male. Then you will produce some big puppies, and some correct-sized puppies. If you double on a fault, you will probably reproduce it visually in the puppies, and even if it is not visual, it will almost certainly appear in future generations. Equally, if you double on a quality your chances of continuing to visually produce that quality are far greater.

There is no doubt that within the Akita breed, as with all other breeds, certain previously created breeding lines, produce certain general characteristics. Also, certain breeding lines mix together very well and others do not. It is a long, slow haul to discover all the facets of this very complicated business. But the most important factor is honesty. If you as a breeder, discover a problem which appears dominant, you must make the decision not to pursue that particular breeding line. It will not go away just because you want it to. In our own experience, one of the breeding lines we originally imported into Britain gave us some superb characteristics, but they also carried some problems which did cause a certain amount of hardship to the dogs. So the decision had to be made. We do not now breed at all to that line, even though its importation was expensive in terms of money, and there were few other dogs to choose from. Instead we have worked at obtaining the good qualities, by using some relatives which had those qualities but which did not carry the problems. It took longer, and indeed is still going on, but in the end the goal will be reached with the elimination of those undesirable faults. No one deliberately goes out to breed a bad dog, but it does happen. These animals should not be penalised. They should still be loved and accepted, but they should be carefully selected out of your plan. Selection is the key. You can never be absolutely certain of what your mating will produce, but you do have the power to select.

TEMPERAMENT

For a breed as powerful and quick as the Akita, good temperament is of the paramount of importance. We would never breed from any dog, no matter how beautiful and typical, if that particular dog or bitch gave us any cause for concern with regard to its temperament. We have no time for those who wish to produce Akitas which are labelled as "sharp" or excessively dominant or over-protective. There is no excuse for breeding from any Akita which shows signs of unreliable or aggressive temperament. We believe that you can enjoy the natural dominant and protective instincts of the Akita within the confines of a dog that is easy to live with. There is no doubt that temperament type is passed on from parent to offspring, be it good or bad. In our opinion bad temperament is never worth the risk and a bad tempered Akita should never be bred from. We must produce animals which can fit into our society and therefore temperament should be considered, perhaps above all other, when selecting mates.

Having carefully selected the mates, some would say that there is an element of luck. Maybe so, although we prefer to encourage the belief that a man makes his own luck. With careful planning and preparation, your chances of being successful are vastly increased.

THE SEASON

Akitas are fertile animals, and the bitch will usually come into season twice each year, or perhaps on a seven-month cycle. Some do go longer between seasons and, during the bitch's lifetime, she may have times when the gap between two seasons may be much longer, perhaps twelve to fourteen months. But this is where the normality ends. For the season can be the normal three weeks in duration, just a few days, or as long as four or even five weeks. This makes it very difficult to assess the right time for mating when the breaking down of the womb is completed and the new eggs are released.

In normal circumstances you would expect the red-coloured discharge to appear and grow stronger over the first eight days or so. It would then pale and cease altogether between the tenth and the twelfth days, and that would be the sign that the eggs have been released and so mating would take place sometime between the tenth and fourteenth day. However, Akita bitches can be quite contrary, to say the least. A bitch might be ready for mating at nine days, although it is more likely that she errs on the late side, between fourteen and sixteen days, and sometimes she will be as late as twenty-one or twenty-two days.

There is, however, a simple, clinical test. A swab is taken from the vagina area and under the microscope the different cell formations, and the presence of the different types of cells, tell the veterinary surgeon the stage the season has reached. The cell formation changes as the bitch is ready to release the eggs, and this would normally be the sign to arrange the visit to the stud dog. The problem with Akita bitches is that they can reach this stage, display it with their cell changes, and then five days later they will still be at the same stage. You, meanwhile, have taken the bitch to the stud dog and probably had a successful mating, for she may accept the dog. However, the sperm may not live long enough to wait for the day when she actually releases her eggs.

Sometimes the male will not show interest, even though the cell shapes suggest the eggs are about to be released, but often he does. Sometimes you are convinced, because of the vet's report, that your bitch is ready for mating, the dog is willing, but the bitch is not! It is very difficult to assess. Many bitches do have several visits to the male to ensure "hitting the right day". Some visit the veterinary surgeon every day over the period in question in an attempt to see the perfect slide showing the correct combination of cells and their formations. In our opinion, gut feeling is a very acceptable method for deciding when the bitch should be mated, although this does preclude the less experienced breeder. The dog and bitch do tell you a lot if you observe their attitude towards each other, and generally a willing bitch and a keen dog should result in puppies being produced. Certainly the veterinary help is invaluable, especially if your chosen stud dog is miles away. Some people prefer to leave the bitch with the sire's owner to save unnecessary travelling. But this can upset the bitch and she may either not ovulate or she may delay ovulation until she has settled down in her new home. Akita bitches are very sensitive and generally need your support. Dogs can also make mistakes. The scent can be right, but the eggs are not there. The biggest danger is impatience or anxiety on the part of the owner. You must allow nature to take its course.

Once the time is right you can prepare to go ahead. As owners of valuable stud dogs, we always insist that any bitch brought for mating, and that includes our own, is tested for any vaginal or womb infection, prior to the mating. This not only safeguards the male, it will also tell you the physical state of health of the bitch. There are many people who attempt to force-mate a bitch who appears to be unreceptive. In fact, the bitch often knows best and she may be suffering from a vaginal infection. The chances are that an infected bitch will not produce puppies, so a swab test will not only save you a lot of time, it will prevent the risk of passing on infection and the disappointment of no puppies being born, not to mention the payment of the stud fee. In these days, when there is such a vast number of dogs around, infections are very common. But if the bitch is tested early enough (we usually test about the second or third day of season), you have a chance to cure the problem before the mating time comes round.

THE MATING

This can be an extremely robust affair. You have two very heavy and powerful animals. In our experience it is not wise to allow them to mate unattended. The power and weight of the dog could cause the bitch to collapse, resulting in a broken leg or a rupture. If it is a maiden bitch, she may be frightened once the dog is tied and swells, possibly causing her pain. You may have a dog that likes to be supervised and handled, or he may wish to perform all by himself. Either way you should be there, either in the forefront or discreetly in the distance, ready to support when necessary.

Irreparable damage can be done when dogs and bitches are left together, with fights developing because the dog is too amorous too soon, and the bitch is trying to ward him off. Strangely enough, most males of most breeds will not attack a bitch who is aggressively warding off the attentions of the male. The dog will accept her wishes, albeit reluctantly, and will eventually back-off until another day. But Akita males will most certainly attack a bitch which shows any sign of aggression. This is a difficult situation, but it has to be accepted as being an integral part of the breed. Obviously, it is best to get the timing right, for a natural mating is far superior to one that is forced; and a happy bitch, eagerly awaiting the advances of a keen and excited male, is the best scenario for all parties.

After reading this, you may wonder how any puppies are produced at all. But of course, they are. There are many times when all goes well, but it is important to be aware of the problems that could arise. In any case, advice is usually very freely given by those with more experience, and you should always seek it. When the mating is satisfactorily concluded, go and celebrate with a good, stiff drink. You will probably need it!

CARE DURING PREGNANCY

Caring for an Akita bitch during pregnancy is basically commonsense. She should be watched carefully and made as comfortable and happy as possible. You should ensure that she has a dry bed, ample clean drinking water and regular feeds of good quality. For the first five weeks she will probably behave quite normally. She may have her "off" days. She may be extra hungry. She may display a slight change in temperament and be more careful how she carries herself, but so long as she is obviously healthy and happy, that is all that matters.

As soon as you suspect that she is pregnant, it is a good idea to contact your vet so he can enter the date of the expected birth in his diary and monitor the bitch's progress. Akitas do not carry much water with their puppies, nevertheless a considerable amount of weight will have to be carried as the weeks progress. It is generally not advisable to give lots of extra food in the early weeks. Experience has taught us that overloading a bitch with food will put weight on her puppies, and she will also put on extra weight. This causes two problems. Firstly, she will not exercise so well, and so she will not be keeping her muscles toned up. Secondly, the puppies will be fat, which means they will be larger and will experience a more difficult passage down the birth canal. And when they are born, they will be fat and lazy.

It is far better to have an active mother and lean, vigorous puppies, who will fight to get to the teats to fill themselves with that all-important mother's first milk. We have found the best policy is to feed a balanced diet with an increase in food after about five weeks. Naturally the future mum will be hungrier, but rest assured that whatever food you give to her she will pass on to her unborn babies before she takes it herself. She is a natural in parental care. Additives in the form of calcium and perhaps iron are a good idea, again after the five-week deadline. These days most foods are carefully balanced and numerous additives should not be needed. Indeed, the general view is that they can do more harm than good. But if the bitch suggests that she may have a deficiency, you should take her to the vet so that proper tests and analysis can be undertaken.

Akita bitches "hide" their puppies very well until at least five weeks, more often six. They may show no signs at all that they are pregnant, and this can be extremely annoying to the owners, who obviously want to know if they are to expect a litter so they can make the necessary preparations. Probably the best indication is a swelling of the bitch's teats. From as early as three weeks these can "pop", or enlarge slightly and become pinker in appearance. In our experience this is the only "sure" sign. Ultra-sound scanning can also give a definite diagnosis, but this is costly and sometimes the hair on the bitch's side or underside has to be removed.

Your bitch may show signs of thickening in the rib or loin earlier, but it is most unlikely. Akita bitches do not generally carry their babies across their loin like most breeds. They hide them under their ribs and then later "drop" them and carry them in the belly, rather like a cow carries its calf. Whether you observe positive signs or not, it is wise to contact your vet and book the expected date of birth into his diary so he will be available if necessary.

Seven weeks into the pregnancy, introduce the bitch to her whelping place. A suitably sized box should be prepared and the absolute minimum measurements for this would be about 4ft 6ins by 3ft. This will allow the bitch to lie fully stretched on her side. The box can certainly be larger, but not so big as to allow the puppies to crawl away from their mother and so get lost. Make sure the bitch is happy with the box and its position. After a few days she will welcome the peace, quiet and solitude of this area and so will accept it as the natural place when the time comes to give birth. If she is at all unhappy you must give in to her and make other arrangements. She probably has a good reason for not wanting things the way you do. So listen to her and adjust. She may accept the box, and then on the day of whelping, she changes her mind and wants to go somewhere else. Again, you must give in to her request. She may return to the box after she has had her first puppy, but let her decide. It is worth all the upheaval to have a happy, contented bitch who comes through her pregnancy successfully and delivers her puppies safely, without causing you — or herself — any undue anxiety.

CHAPTER TEN

WHELPING

WHEN the big day finally arrives, are you ready, are you properly and fully prepared? Remember, it is at this time that your Akita mum most needs your support. Of course, she is quite capable of giving birth herself, and she should be left to get on with things, as far as possible. Your role should be as an observer, ready to help if needed. It is worth bearing in mind that you have instigated this situation, so you must accept responsibility for her welfare.

Before the event, certain items should be made ready. They are: the whelping box, plenty of warm towels, which will be needed to clean the bitch and rub the puppies, a household thermometer to test the temperature of the floor of the box, a clinical thermometer to take the bitch's temperature, a sterilised pair of small scissors to cut the umbilical cords, an antiseptic disinfectant in a small bowl to clean your hands and the scissors, clean, white paper to line the bottom of the box, which should be changed as necessary throughout the whelping, a cardboard box (about 2ft square and 5ins deep), complete with hot-water bottle and towel covering for the newly-born puppies while the bitch is giving birth to later arrivals. You should also have some form of heating, either a radiator or an overhead infra-red lamp, to ensure that the box is adequately warm, and a clock to monitor the time between contractions and births.When you have assembled all these items, you can relax. Your job is now to be as patient and attentive as possible.

Akita bitches, like most other bitches, seem to prefer to whelp at night, so you should be prepared to lose a night's sleep. A comfortable chair in the whelping room is a good idea, but take care not to doze off. Not everyone has the facility for a separate whelping room in their home, and they will use a kennel or a corner of the kitchen. We feel that the bitch needs to be close at hand, but not disturbed, and so our own room is adjacent to the kitchen, closed off but with a viewing window so that we can monitor what is going on without disturbing mother or babies once they arrive. The room is heated by a radiator, which removes the chill during the summer and in winter this is supplemented by an overhead infra-red lamp. This means we can adjust the temperature in a variety of ways.

Puppies like to be kept warm, at around 70 degrees Fahrenheit for the first few days. But take care extra care and use the room thermometer. Place it on the bottom of the box to test the heat. Remember that the bitch's head will be about eighteen inches higher than the box bottom, and that the puppies will receive a considerable amount of warmth from their mother's body. If the bitch is too hot, she will feel uncomfortable and will pant. The pups may try to move away from her to cool down, and this is not a satisfactory situation. If the room is too cold, the puppies will become chilled, especially during the first couple of days when they will be constantly cleaned by mum, who may have a discharge which keeps on wetting the puppies. If the temperature drops too low, the puppies will huddle together to try and keep warm. The picture you should see is a comfortable, calm mum with a row of sleeping, contented pups, lying snug and warm beside their mother.

In our experience, Akita bitches do not go to the full sixty-three days of gestation. It is far more common for them to whelp on the sixtieth or sixty-first day. On the fifty-ninth day or later, you will see that the bitch is becoming increasingly unsettled. She may have difficulty getting comfortable and be restless. Does this mean that early labour has begun? It can do, but very often this behaviour means that you have to wait another twenty-four hours before the labour starts. However, you cannot afford to take a chance on it. Any change whatsoever in the bitch's behaviour should be monitored carefully. We have a very sensitive baby alarm system which we connect from the side of the whelping box to the side of our bed, so if we feel a little apprehensive at bedtime, we can switch on the alarm and still get some sleep. The slightest noise from the box will trigger the alarm, and so we can then investigate. If things appear to be happening in the daytime, the alarm can be connected to whichever room you are working in, and so you are kept fully informed without wasting endless hours just sitting and watching.

Once it is clear that labour has begun, it is time to down tools and go into the whelping room. But first, remember to telephone the vet to notify him that labour has begun. He can then be at the ready if you need him. We would never leave a bitch to whelp on her own — both for her sake, and in case the new-born puppies need help. From a personal viewpoint, we would not like to miss a birth, for no matter how many times we have witnessed this miracle, it still fills us with awe and wonder. There is no greater thrill than the moment when that first new-born puppy bundle drops into your hand. It is the beginning. You had a hand in its creation. You can only wonder at its future.

As soon as the first puppy has been born, telephone the vet to inform him that whelping has commenced. Akita bitches whelp as they do everything else: quietly, calmly, and with a sense of purpose. The early stages of labour can be missed by the inexperienced eye as there is seldom a sign of breaking waters, blood discharge or extreme pain. A certain sign is the clear, very sticky mucus at the vagina. This means the seal on the womb is broken and the puppies are not too far away.

Akitas do seem to have a high threshold for pain. The early, less strong contractions cannot always be seen as the puppy begins its journey into the birth canal. The bitch will, however show signs which are unmistakable. She will sit, then lie, then sit, then lie. Turn round, reach for her vaginal area, droop her eyes, and bring her ears close together. All these signs suggest that she is experiencing some pain. As time progresses you will see definite contractions. They will be very powerful and generally quite long in duration. Monitor the length of time between contractions: as with humans, they come closer together as the moment of birth approaches. Once you see this type of contraction, the puppies are very near. We have known many instances when only three contractions have been seen before the puppy has arrived. So you have to be very watchful and be on hand.

The birth of the first puppy may be painful enough for the bitch to cry out. You must comfort her, although she will be more concerned with what is happening behind than anything you are doing. If it is her first time, she may be frightened and she will be comforted by your presence. Make a final check that everything is ready, and then with one last push that small, or rather quite large bundle, appears. Hopefully it will be a neat package of puppy in the birth bag, attached by the cord to the afterbirth. Now, whether it is the bitch's first or last litter, whether it is the first or last pup to arrive,the chances are that your bitch will be more intent on cleaning herself than attending to the puppy. It is therefore up to you to break the bag with your fingers and cut the cord, about one inch from the puppy with your scissors or with your fingernails.

Never take the puppy away from where it is lying, alongside the bitch. Remember, it is her puppy, not yours. Whatever you do must be done literally under her nose. Never mind if you are uncomfortable, stretching over the box, or whatever. The bitch and her puppy are the important ones. You are merely the catalyst, if you like, aiding the outcome of this wonderful experiment. When you place the puppy under the bitch's tongue, she will be quick to realise that it belongs to her and she will start licking it. This is the best stimulus any puppy can have. Rub the puppy with a towel, especially around the nose and mouth to remove any excess mucus, and rub the body to stimulate movement.

Most breeds cry out when rubbed vigorously. That way you know they are alive and breathing: squeals mean the lungs will be fully extended so you know all is well. Akita puppies, however, may make no sound at all. We well remember our very first litter. There was the puppy, wriggling, but not a sound. We rubbed and rubbed and still no sound. But of course, these are Akitas. They are silent. And so are their puppies. So do not worry if there is no sound. You can see the ribcage moving and you will be able to see them wriggle!

It is unlikely that there will be much water arriving with the puppy; there may not be any. Akita bitches do not carry the gallons of water it seems that bitches in other breeds carry. The births, like the dogs and their daily habits, are clean and tidy. One thing to watch, though, is the afterbirth. You must count the puppies and the afterbirths. There should be one for each, and the afterbirth should arrive with each puppy. But this does not always happen. Sometimes the afterbirth from puppy number two will arrive during the contractions for puppy number three, and so on. Sometimes you may not see it arrive, as the bitch may eat it as she cleans herself. There is always the possibility that one afterbirth or some part of it is left inside.This can be dealt with later by means of an injection by your veterinary surgeon, which will ensure the afterbirth is evacuated by normal contractions.

After the first puppy has arrived there will probably be a period, it may be a few minutes, it may be half-an-hour or even longer, when the new mother can tend her baby. It will be cleaned and cosseted endlessly. It may naturally scramble towards the teat. It may need your assistance to suckle. Akita puppies are very willing to suckle very soon after birth, but if it needs your help, make sure you keep the puppy in contact with the mother at all times. Do not pick it up. Slide it along, easing gently. Suckling seems to induce contractions for the next puppy. If the bitch is active during this time, moving around to position herself for the next arrival, you may be able to place the puppy in the cardboard box, heated by the hot-water bottle and towel covering. This box, though, must be placed so the bitch can reach into it. She may object strongly to having the puppy removed, in which case you should leave the puppy with her and ensure that it is safe and not stepped on or lain on during the next delivery. As soon as you have more than one puppy, it will be easier to remove all but one puppy from the mother, without too much distress. If she can reach the puppies and she can still tend them, she will usually accept the arrangement. It certainly makes it safer for the one you leave with the mother, and we suggest this should be the most recently born. While the later puppies are being born, check the first-borns regularly to ensure they are warm and breathing without any mucussy sound. Your bitch may be offered water at this time, but she will probably refuse it. Do not give her any food.

The length of time between puppies can vary enormously. The puppies may come one-at-a-time, in regular half-hour intervals. They may come in pairs: one puppy followed by another, perhaps fifteen minutes later, and then a long gap of an hour or hour-and-a-half and two more puppies arrive. The first three or four may come reasonably close together, and then you may have a long wait for the rest. There is no set pattern, and no need to be alarmed. The bitch must be closely watched for her attitude. She should be quite contented between births. She may even sleep, which is almost unheard of in other breeds. The time gap may extend to four hours or more, although any interval longer than two hours should be reported to the vet. The condition known as Inertia is not unknown in Akitas, indeed it occurs fairly regularly. The difficulty is recognising the difference between Inertia and resting. So long as the bitch appears calm and relaxed, there is no need to doubt her welfare. However, any sign of excessive straining, pain, strong panting, shaking or scurrying around, should be closely investigated.

Equally, any sign of absolute apathy on her part should cause alarm bells to ring. Her eyes will give you the clearest sign. If she looks frightened or miserable, the chances are that she is experiencing difficulties. You must read the signs. A puppy could be wedged in the birth canal, causing pain and distress and also preventing the later puppies from being delivered. Remember that once those puppies up above have broken away from the lining of the womb, they are on their own. They need to be born as soon as possible. If you have any doubts at all, ring your vet. If his help is required, then it is probably better to take your bitch to the surgery. The chances are that if something is seriously wrong, the surgery will be far better equipped than your home. Sometimes the vet can come to your house and administer an injection which will hasten the birth of the later puppies, particularly if the bitch has become tired. The injection is the hormone which stimulates contractions. However, if there is a real problem, such as a wedged puppy or Inertia, then a caesarian section will be the only solution. When this is carried out by a competent veterinary surgeon, this form of delivery, whether it is for all or part of a litter, should be one hundred per cent successful. It will be just as wonderful to see those little bundles freed from their mother's body and then placed into your hands on a warm towel, and rubbed into life. It is hard work but very rewarding. Your bitch should recover perfectly; and she does not appear to mind the pain of the incision.

When the litter has been safely delivered, you can celebrate with a well-earned cup of tea and offer the new mum some food and and a chance to empty. Again, let her decide. She should be gently cleaned but not disturbed too much. A thorough cleaning job can be done the following day. This should also bring a visit from the vet, who can check the bitch to ensure the womb has contracted and that there is no sign of a bad discharge or any other problem. Some vets give petuetrin and penicillin to ensure the womb is cleared and to ward off infection. It is a matter of choice, which depends on the circumstances of the birth and the advice of your vet. A normal, clean birth, with no complications, would not usually warrant any medicine, but a careful watch should be maintained over the next few days.

CHAPTER ELEVEN

REARING

REARING should be looked on as one of the most important tasks in breeding. You are not only responsible for feeding and nurturing your new Akita puppies, but you are also playing a large part in their overall development — their temperament, their attitude to life and their ability to cope and fit into society. The term 'husbandry' is rarely used in the dog world, but in many ways it is a more apt description than 'rearing', for it encompasses all these vital elements.

The ability to rear puppies is an art. It can be taught, but only to those who are prepared to dedicate themselves to endless hours of watching and monitoring. A natural mother is a boon to any new baby, and a natural helper, in the form of you, the breeder, is invaluable. The mother will rely on instinct; you will have to acquire your expertise through experience — and through your ability to learn from experience. We have been breeding puppies for a long time and still we do not know it all. Each pregnancy, whelping, rearing and litter is different, and there is always something new to learn. There are the basics which apply to all breeds, but the Akita, as we have said many times before, is special.

THE FIRST FEW DAYS

After the delivery, mother and puppies are best left on their own, while you get some rest. When you return to the whelping box you should find a contented scene, with the mother busily attending to her babies. By now, the puppies should be sucking strongly and their coats should have dried out and will look like shining velvet. Approach carefully, so as not to disturb the mother. She needs to practise the art of not stepping on her puppies, so give her the chance to leave the box calmly and sedately, if she wishes to do so. This will give you a good opportunity to inspect her for any discharge and make sure that she can stand easily. You may have to clean her, although she will probably have done a good job of this herself. She should also be offered food and a drink at this stage.

The bitch will want to return to her puppies as quickly as possible. Help her to position them, and then you may begin your inspection. We do not weigh our puppies, although many people do. We do not see the point, because even if they do not weigh the ideal weight, there is little you can do about it. It is far better to let nature take its course. In the first few days all the puppies will feed well, whatever their size. It is only later that a smaller one may need help to hang on to the fullest teat, so that it is not pushed aside by larger puppies.

The first few days should be ones of watchfulness, though you should also handle the puppies, so they get used to the touch of the human hand. You will need to move them to change their bedding, and if they know your touch right from the start, they will accept it as part of their life. Never take a puppy away from the whelping box; whatever you do must be done under the mother's nose, just as it was during the delivery. After all, they are her babies and she wants them. You are just the helper. Puppies are very quick to tell mother, and you, if there is anything wrong. An ill or unhappy puppy will not be contented. Sometimes the mother will tell you the puppy is "rejected" by pushing it away. You may not be able to see any problem, but in our experience the bitch knows what she is doing. It is a difficult situation, but any rejected puppy should be seen by your vet to try to establish what is wrong.

Given that they are all healthy you should check that all the puppies can feed easily. Place your little finger on to the roof of the mouth to ensure there is no cleft palate. Feel the rear legs to check for the dew-claws. These may or may not be present. If they are, they may be large, small, double or minute. Dew-claws on an Akita can be located in the usual place, just above the rear foot on the inside of the leg, or sometimes right at the bottom almost on the last toe. They are sometimes so small that you can miss them on a quick inspection. The best way to check is to gently rub your fingernail from the toe up the inside of the leg to the hock joint. Repeat this process each day for the first five days, in case a claw has grown during that time. We always ask the vet to remove dew-claws at five days, and not before. It is not until five days that the blood gains clotting properties, and so then the operation can be done without causing bleeding and minimising the risk of infection. Keep an eye on the umbilical cord to ensure it dries up properly and that there are no signs of swelling or rupture. The whelping box should be kept warm, at about 70 degrees Farenheit for the first few days.

CARING FOR THE MOTHER

The mother is feeding the puppies and therefore her diet is extremely important. Although during her pregnancy you have not given her excessive amounts of food, you may now feed as much as you like. She will tell you what she needs. During the first few days she will not be ravenous. The puppies are small and she will have made ample milk for their needs. A high-protein diet and plenty of water is the best formula for producing milk, and Akita mothers produce what appears to be gallons of it. We have never known such a plentiful supply in any other breed. As the days go by, the flow will increase and as the puppies grow stronger they will enjoy it immensely. We would supplement her diet with a little natural calcium, such as bonemeal, but nothing else unless the vet advised it. Porridge and milk do not produce milk; all they do is fill the mother's stomach without giving any goodness to the puppies.

The mother's health and well-being are most important. She should be inspected frequently. Her teats should be examined to ensure they are not damaged or swollen. There should be no swelling or hardness of the areas around the teats which might lead to milk fever (mastitis). The vulva should gradually become smaller, but it will be very tender as it is undoubtedly bruised from the birth. This will not be visible because of the dark colouring. Any discharge, other than a small amount of mucus-stained clear red from blood, should be reported to your vet and investigated. Any odour of any kind should also be investigated.

The bitch's mental health should be monitored. She should appear well and be happy in her eyes and expression. She should eat and drink almost normally, although she will need more water and you should ensure she has an adequate supply. Staining from the discharge should be wiped away and a mild disinfectant should be used in an attempt to deter any flies. Care should be taken not to mask her natural smell, as this is how the puppies know her. Keep a regular check on the toilet of both mother and babies. A common occurrence is to observe a puppy grunting unhappily, suffering from constipation. Mother may also suffer from this, as her normal exercise has been drastically reduced. A small drink of warm milk, sweetened with sugar, or ideally with natural honey, should ease the problem. If you make the drink too sweet, you will get the opposite problem, so it is easy to regulate until you get it right.

THE GROWTH RATE

Phenomenal — that is the only word to describe it. Each morning when you visit the puppies you will not be able to believe that it is the same family that you left last night. It really is that astounding. The puppies grow so rapidly that they make enormous demands on their mother. She must be watched continually for any signs of distress, unsteadiness or shaking, which could lead to mastitis or eclampsia. If you observe any of these symptoms, you should contact your vet immediately. The mother's health is vital, for she is the one who is taking care of the puppies. Without her, you would have a formidable task on your hands, which you could never fulfil as well as her.

ONE WEEK OLD

In less than one week the puppies will have doubled in size. They will be gaining strength and will be able to move around the box quickly and with purpose. The head shape will change and they will begin to look like miniature Akitas. The legs become thick and strong, the coat plushy. It is easy to see the angulation of the rear legs at this stage, and it is the best time to assess this particular standard point as it will not be apparent again until the pups are four to five months old. Many breeders keep a written record of each puppy and include all their findings. This is a good idea, but generally you will remember each puppy and will have names for them like "dumpling" or "black patch" or "little ears" For one of the joys of an Akita litter is that all the puppies are so different.

TWO WEEKS OLD

At some time after ten days the puppies will begin to open their eyes, although we have found that fourteen to eighteen days is more the norm. How nice it is to see those little faces develop character as the eyes open! They are quite beautiful. The head has a definite dome now, and the puppies have broadened out to be very round in appearance. They are already difficult to pick up with one hand — though it is better to handle them as little as possible as this can lead to tummy-ache. You have to curb your affection and take pleasure in just sitting and watching.

THREE WEEKS OLD

The three-week stage means you have little individuals on your hands. The puppies are just discovering each other and will try to sit up and nuzzle the noses of their brothers and sisters. Soon they will stand and move across the box on their legs, although they are a bit wobbly at first.

It is important that the bedding you are using gives them a firm grip. The proprietary brands of veterinary bedding are excellent for the first few weeks, but we have found that it is so soft that it can cause poor foot condition. A harder surface will mean the puppies can grip and flex their toe muscles to give tighter feet. Paper can sometimes be slippery and a single sheet of thin blanket, fastened down, is an excellent base.

FOUR WEEKS OLD

Very soon the puppies will need more space and they are ready to leave the nest. An area outside the whelping box should be made available. Mother will leave the the pups from time to time, particularly when food is on offer, for she will be continually starving and should be given food in quantities which may be as high as four times the norm. Care should be taken so that she does not scour, and the food should be adjusted accordingly. She should always be allowed to return to the box to feed her puppies.

The pups will find their first excursion outside the nest an alarming experience. They will whine and cower down when they find themselves on a new and strange-smelling surface. But with sufficient encouragement from their mother and from you (probably on your hands and knees on the floor!), they will overcome their apprehension, and their natural curiosity will take over. These visits should be short at first, and the puppies should not be allowed to get wet or dirty. As the days go by, they will cry out to be allowed this new freedom, and when they are about four weeks old they should be waddling around quite happily. They will also very quickly develop clean toilet habits, and you will find that they will wait until they are taken from the box before they empty. In our experience, this habit is very much more pronounced in Akitas than any other breed, and they should be thanked for it, as it makes life so much easier!

WEANING

Akita bitches will feed and indeed demand to feed their puppies until they are about eight weeks of age. They continue to produce large quantities of milk and the fullness of their teats stimulates them to feed their babies. The more they feed, the more milk is produced, and so eventually you have to give a helping hand. Obviously, the pups will not be so keen to feed from their mother once you start feeding them. It is difficult to judge the right time to wean puppies. It should be when they look fine but you have the feeling that a solid meal would give them that extra strength to stand and move around. It does not depend on the precise age of the litter: the puppies could be three and a half weeks old or four and a half weeks old. But when you see the puppies feeding fiercely, emptying the teat and quickly moving to the next, you will see that mealtimes are developing into a frenzied search for food, and it is time to start weaning.

We always wean on to solid food. We have found that Akita puppies do not take kindly to any milk except their mother's. We recommend that you use very finely minced beef and place a small amount on your fingertips and allow the puppy to sniff it. Within seconds it takes the morsel into his mouth. The pup will soon realise it not only tastes good but it makes him feel good to have a nice, full tummy. A teaspoonful is ample for the first two or three times, usually at breakfast and tea. Again, keep a close eye on the toilet and use the sweeteners to regulate. Remember what they always tell us humans: "Healthy on the inside means healthy on the outside!"

It is a good idea to keep the mother away for longer periods when you are weaning. Although you are providing food, the puppies will still need their mother's milk, which contains the natural antibodies against disease. If she is kept away, the puppies will be more ready to accept your food and the mother will have the chance to replenish her milk store. She may object initially, but her absences should be increased gradually. If you feed the puppies before she does, they will not draw on her so hard when she returns.

FIVE WEEKS OLD

It is important to appreciate the dramatic increase in food you should give the puppies. The quantity will double almost daily from that first day until ten days, and then it will slow down to an increase of about 25 per cent to 50 per cent per week. Definite quantities cannot be quoted and it depends on the type of food you are feeding. Some breeders prefer a complete food, it is a matter of personal choice, and we would not wish to impose our own chosen diet on anyone else. However, it is important to bear in mind that dogs are carnivores and therefore they like to eat meat. We feed meat in some shape or form, with other items carefully selected to give a balanced diet. We have never had a finicky eater, either puppy or adult. For those who wish to feed a complete food, make sure you refer to the manufacturer's instructions and, where puppies are concerned, speak to the company's representative to gain as much information as possible from other breeders they have supplied.

By the time they are five or six weeks old, most puppies will have stopped feeding from their mother. This is the time for you to add two meals to their daily menu — lunch and supper (although mother will still give the supper if she is still spending the night with her babies). We recommend the extra meals should be: scrambled egg (about one quarter egg per puppy) mixed with natural honey and water, or full cream rice-pudding, or plain powdered milk, sweetened with honey. But eggs should only be fed once, or at the most twice, per week. You can also introduce hard biscuits, to help to exercise the jaws and teeth, which will be very sharp by now. We have found that baby-rusks are a great favourite. We would also add natural calcium in the form of bonemeal. Additives should not be given if supplements are already included in a complete diet. Any looseness of toilet will be the result of too much milk, and not from too much meat.

CARE OF THE GROWING BROOD

Sharp teeth and nails can cause harm to the mother, and the puppies' nails should be carefully trimmed when necessary. If this is done early enough, the puppies will not object. The mother's teats should be inspected regularly to ensure there are no abrasions from either teeth or nails. If there are any, apply an antiseptic cream, which will not harm the puppies. Long nails can also be a potential danger to other puppies during playtimes, which get increasingly rough as the pups grow older.

WORMING

This is the subject of much debate. Many breeders worm from as early as ten days and then continue worming at regular intervals during the first year. Others do not worm at all unless they see signs of infestation. It is a matter of personal choice, but it should always be done with a preparation from your veterinary surgeon. Never worm a sick puppy; a few worms will not do as much harm as administering this medicine, which, after all, is a poison. Equally, never worm a puppy when you are changing its diet. If you are in the process of weaning or introducing new things to the puppies' or the mother's diet, do not worm. Any change in diet means a change in the "bugs" inside the system which break down the food. It could spell disaster if you introduce "poison" at the same time as a request for different "bugs" to cope with the food. It has been found that parvo-virus nasties, in particular, love this sort of atmosphere. Even if you suspect worms, wait. Almost all puppies have worms to some degree, and

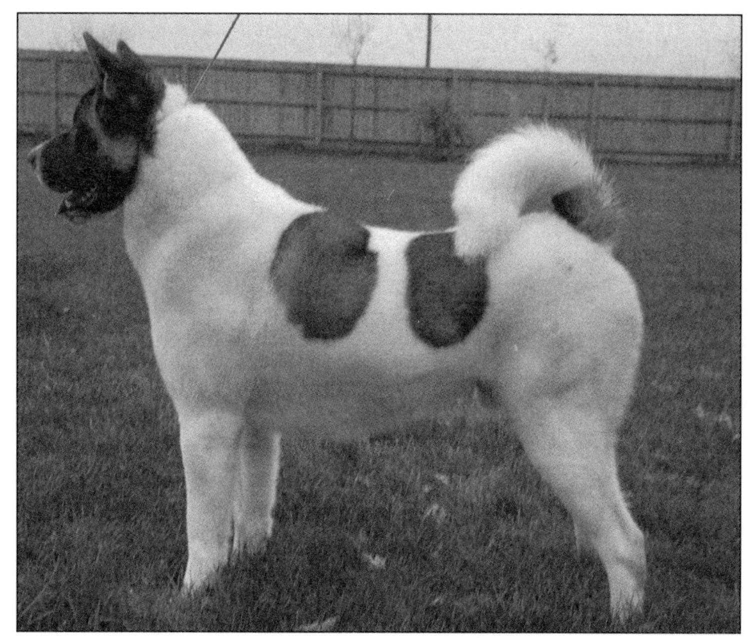

The Sire: Kato, a brown and white pinto with a black head.

The Dam: Jezebel, silver and white, black overlay and black head.

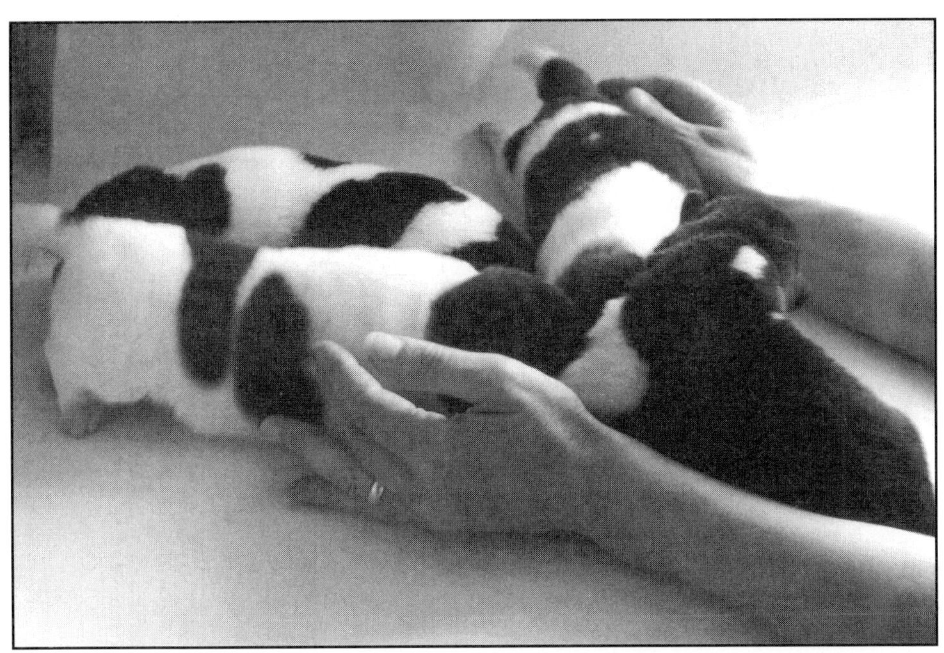

Their puppies: four males at one week old. They all appear black and white at this stage.

Four males at five weeks old, getting used to the great outdoors.

At eight weeks: Black and white pinto, black head.

At eight weeks: Black and white pinto, black head.

At eight weeks: Silver with black overlay, black head.

At eight weeks: Silver with black overlay, Irish spotted markings, black mask, white blaze.

the worst they can do is rob the puppy of some of its food. You can easily eradicate worms in a day or so, before they have had the chance to do any harm.

SIX WEEKS OLD

As the puppies grow older, they should be introduced to the outside world in preparation for their departure. You should give them the opportunity to learn by exploring, starting with the garden and then allowing them into the house to get used to the feel of carpet beneath their feet, the noise of the television and telephone, and other everyday sounds. You should talk to the pups so they learn the difference in your voice when you are saying "Hello my little ones, come and play," and "No, that's naughty."

You should wash them to keep them clean, brush them, and make them behave in an orderly manner when they become too boisterous. It is a matter of personal choice whether you allow visitors to meet the puppies. It is difficult to say no to a prospective owner, and if they are planning to buy a puppy, they will want to see the litter's development. The best thing to do is to provide a fenced-off area close to the house, so visitors can see the puppies without actual contact. It is so easy to spread disease; you should not be worried about prohibiting a visitor who has been at a show, in contact with other dogs. Insist that all visitors disinfect their feet before coming into the house; after all, it could be their puppy you are protecting. Despite all these precautions, we do feel very strongly that it is the duty of every breeder to socialise their puppies. They are not just commodities to be brought up in a kennel until they are sent on their way. They are little beings with minds which are crying out for information. Make sure that you educate them: it is one of the great joys of rearing a litter.

THE PARTING

By the time the puppies are seven to eight weeks old, they should be fully weaned. Their mother should still be in attendance so that she can play with them and enjoy them, but they should have learnt that there is no milk to be had from her, and they should not pester her. The puppies' education should be well underway and they should have learnt some words and some sounds, like the rustle of the biscuit packet and the clatter of the feeding bowls. They will be emerging as individuals, with their own distinctive characteristics.

Every breeder has their own way of managing the sale of puppies, but we feel that all future homes should have been vetted for suitability. The

Mauraine Caramia: At 13 months, she illustrates that in-breeding can be successful. She is the daughter of a full litter brother and sister mating. Bred, owned and handled by Maurice and Loraine Webb.

puppies should be sent on their way with a diet sheet, a complete run-down on future care, your telephone number, a pedigree and a Kennel Club registration certificate (or a promise of one if there has been a delay). You can decide whether you provide written receipts and agreements. You may also wish to sell or "place" a puppy with the proviso that it should not be used for breeding. There are a number of ways this can be done: some people give written contracts, some withhold registration certificates, some use the Kennel Club facility of endorsing the registration, although this can be lifted by the Kennel Club at their own discretion. Some breeders do not register the puppy. Some provide a veterinary certificate before the puppies leave. Some future owners will insist on a veterinary inspection, in any case. All you can do is to take every safeguard to ensure that the puppies you have bred go to the best possible homes. The greatest reward is when you meet up with one of your pups at a future date and see the dog looking fit and well, and in many instances, it will still recognise you. Although you spend a relatively short time with the puppies, it is an all-important time in their lives and will have a significant bearing on their future welfare.

Kimono: The loveliest puppy we have ever seen, pictured at 12 weeks.

CHAPTER TWELVE

THE RIGHT START

At long last you have brought your Akita puppy home. Now it all begins — the start of your new life together with all the pleasures and joys you are to share. The first important thing to bear in mind is that it is an Akita that you have taken responsibility for. This may seem a very obvious statement to make, but the point is Akita puppies are different from any other breed of dog. Of course, your puppy will do all the things puppies usually do, but there are signs you must watch for that need special attention. These relate to feeding, grooming, health, training, understanding and love; and an early recognition of these special needs will benefit both you and your Akita.

LOVE

Whatever else you may have to do to make your Akita happy, you must always do it with love. For they respond better to love than to any other thing on earth. All aspects of care and training should be practised with firmness, but also with kindness and affection. Even a tap on the nose should be followed by a kiss, so that the puppy — or an adult, for that matter — understands that you were only trying to explain your wishes. The dog needs to know that you still love him and that he is not being punished for things he did not know were wrong. The dog is eager to be taught, and you must take on the role of teacher.

All youngsters have a natural exuberance and sometimes this has to be stemmed, for its own benefit and to protect your property. But the dog must understand that it is not the exuberance that is wrong but the ways in which the exuberance affects other matters. You must always show affection towards your puppy — when offering food, administering medicine, training or at any other time. Affection is infectious. You give

Angela Jackson with Kezmar Storm Trouper. .

it, and you will get it back. Remember, whether you are teaching him new things or chastising him because he has forgotten those things, he loves you, and wants you to love him. This is the best opportunity you will ever have to teach your puppy to respect you. Later on, when your Akita weighs in excess of six or seven stone, he will still believe he is subordinate to you and will respect your wishes.

FEEDING

You will have found out about your puppy's diet at the time of purchase and you should be equipped to give him the food he is used to. Most good breeders will send you away with a diet sheet (and it should be exactly the one they have been feeding, and not one copied from a book and not actually used), plus a quantity of the main food of the puppy's diet so that continuity can be maintained over the first few days. This is important, because a change of geographical area will mean a change in "bugs" around and continuity of food will minimise the risk of upset. You should ensure your puppy is fed regularly; little and often is the order of the day. Four small meals are better than one or two large ones so that weight distribution is kept at an average.

Your puppy will drink a lot of water and this should always be available. Do remember to show the puppy where the bowl is and keep it in the same place. Any change in diet should be undertaken gradually and increases in food intake monitored very carefully. The puppy should look nicely covered; neither too thin and ribby, nor too fat and blown. Each time you increase the food, check that the puppy still looks the same, and you will know you have got it right. Diet is a matter of personal choice, but the puppy does need plenty of protein, calcium and minerals. Overdoing it is, however, just as bad as not doing it at all. So be sensible and check with your vet if you have any worries. Ask other owners and always keep in touch with the breeder.

As your puppy grows, it will naturally cut down on the milky meals until they can be left out altogether. The timing is not important; watch the puppy and be guided by what it is telling you. We feed growing youngsters exactly as we feed our puppies; we just increase the quantities. After all, the formula was fine for babies, and so it should suit growing youngsters. Your puppy may continue with two meals a day until it is twelve month old. (In fact, we feed all our dogs twice daily.) This is a matter of choice; but remember, sensible feeding is the key to your dog enjoying a long and healthy life.

GROOMING

Akita puppies do not need much grooming. The coat is soft and plushy and will not become entangled or matted, even if it is left untended. But it does need to be kept clean, both by shampooing and brushing. It is also advisable to teach your puppy at an early age to accept your attentions. It will look and feel better after a thorough grooming; but beware — if you thought the proverbial eel was slippery, just wait!

It is important that you teach your puppy to behave by showing kindness as well as firmness. The puppy must respect your wishes, but you must be gentle and try to make the episode enjoyable. The easiest method is to hold the dog underneath the chest with one hand and brush with the other, keeping a firm grip and always holding on with at least one hand.

At about sixteen weeks of age, much of the puppy undercoat, or camouflage coat as it is often called, will be shed. Regular brushing is essential at this time to ensure there is no build-up of dirt and old hair. It takes a few weeks for the coat to fully change but by about five months you will see the true Akita coat and colour emerging. The coat will be livelier, brighter, and a strong evidence of top coat will be both seen and felt. Now you have the makings of a true Akita. Keep up the brushing and cleaning, and your duckling will emerge into a swan.

HEALTH CARE

Skin Problems

Closely connected with feeding and grooming, there are certain things to watch for that are peculiar to the puppy stage. By far the most common is skin problems. Almost all Akitas suffer from what is commonly known as nappy rash, which will appear on the belly. This can occur at any time between ten weeks to ten months and always needs immediate attention. These skin problems are not so much disorders as imperfections, but they can cause distress, so the dog should be checked almost daily for any signs.

There are various remedies which work very well, so long as they are administered in the early stages. Certain gels and shampoos are effective, and some of these work better than remedies bought from the vet. Normally we would always advise a visit to the vet, whatever the problem, because he is the expert. However, in this instance, the vet may not have the best remedies available. The Japanese Akita Club of Great Britain operates its 24-hour Hotline service to help with all problems relating to the Akita. It has information on these skin medicines, which have been tried and tested by Akita owners. If the skin problem does occur, you should always mention it to your vet to ensure that it is not some other problem, such as infestation by fleas, which would need veterinary treatment.

Worms

Puppies are usually wormed between five and seven weeks of age, so your pup should have been wormed before you brought it home. There should be no need to worm again until after the course of immunization. Even if you suspect worms, it is unlikely that the problem will be so bad that you need to worm earlier.

Immunization

With the advances in medicine, there are now many ways to immunize against disease and different times when this should be done. You should follow the advice of your vet, for he will be caring for the dog for the foreseeable future. It is important that the full course of immunization is given, so that your puppy has the best protection. There has been no evidence of Akitas reacting badly to any of these injections, and most dogs will not even notice the prick of the needle as it does its job.

Sleep

This may seem a strange topic to discuss - but not so far as Akita puppies are concerned. They really do need a lot of sleep, and it is important that they get it. The temptation is to keep your puppy on the go all day, playing with it, taking it for walks and showing it off to friends and neighbours. But the puppy is growing at a very fast rate and it needs a quiet place to go, where it can rest in peace. It will sleep for the majority of the day, if it is allowed to. Sometimes you will need to put the puppy in its bed and ignore the howls for a few minutes until it is ready to settle down to a much-needed sleep. A puppy will always want to carry on playing, but you should decide when enough is enough and give it the opportunity to have the rest which is so important to its development.

Ears

The only real problem you will ever get with an Akita's ears is when they are "lifting". In the normal course of events, this transition from drooped to erect ears occurs at some stage between five and twenty weeks. However, ears can lift as late as eight months, and if this happens, you

A puppy's ears can go through some strange phases before they lift, as this 14-week-old illustrates.

will have many anxious days wondering if they will ever lift at all. The ears of an adult Akita should be firmly erect, as described in the breed standard. In our experience, the quality of the ear, in every respect, is genetic, and therefore they will lift of their own accord as, and when, they wish to do so.

As a general rule, we would say that if your puppy does not have erect ears by the time it is fourteen weeks old, you should call for help. There are certain support materials which can help in some cases, and it does seem better to give a helping hand than to leave everything to providence. The problem is, you will never know if the ears would have lifted without help, and therefore you may be breeding in a disposition which you do not really want. However, there are some instances when no matter what you do to help, the ears will remain in the dropped position. If you are worried, check with the vet to ensure there is no infection causing discomfort in the ear, and then check the teeth. We have found on many occasions that teething can play havoc with ear development.

Teeth

Again, Akitas do not experience any particular problems, except during puppyhood. Akitas cut their new teeth very late. Even at five to six months old, you may still find baby teeth. Careful monitoring is essential, especially when the canine teeth are coming through. Sometimes the baby teeth refuse to drop out and the new canine tooth will push its way through and jam in the old one. Keep a close watch and see what happens. If your puppy reaches five-and-a-half-months or so and the new tooth is wedged in with the old, the vet will be able to sort it out in no time. Don't ignore the problem: it is a simple procedure to set matters right and it will certainly be appreciated by your puppy.

Growth

Just as with new-born puppies, the growth-rate of youngsters is quite phenomenal and so the growing bones, tendons and tissues are very vulnerable. In the wild, the youngsters would enjoy complete freedom and run around without interference from humans or household obstacles. The pup may try to run up and down after you; it has to negotiate steps to and from the garden; shoes might be left lying about; all these are potential hazards for a youngster finding its feet. In the same way that you are caring for the growing pup by feeding the correct diet, you must also do your best to ensure that it develops without risk of injury.

Kiskas Ty-Ffoon: At 12-weeks and looking in good proportion.

Kiskas Ty-Ffoon: At four-and-a-half months, showing irregular growth and dropped ears.

Kiskas Ty-Ffoon, owned by the Pearson family, at three years old. He fulfilled all his early promise, despite the awkward adolescent stage.

HOUSING

We would never bring up a puppy in an outside kennel. There are several reasons for this: the dog will be unhappy, it will get dirty, it will not get to know you, it will not learn anything. Consequently we would always bring up a puppy within the home atmosphere. It will benefit from being part of the family; you can keep it clean; it will learn to understand your habits and actions; and it will will come on a treat!

We are not saying that the puppy must not go outside. If you have a lot of dogs, you have to provide outside accommodation. Our own dogs do live outside (save the eleven-year-old Welsh Springer Champion who rules the roost!), but the youngsters are reared indoors to learn toilet training, household noises, and all the usual comings and goings of domestic life. Anyway, you don't want to miss all the funny things your puppy will get up to: this is part of the joy of owning an Akita!

CHILDREN

Akitas love children, and children will love Akitas, especially when they are puppies. But there is a danger. If you have children, you must ensure that they appreciate that the puppy is a live animal with feelings and desires. It is not a soft toy to be pulled about and kicked around. It must be allowed to behave in a sensible manner, and so must your children. There will certainly be times when you must step in and separate the two. As your Akita grows, it will love and protect your children as part of its family. This bond will only be formed if the dog grows up respecting the children, and vice versa.

TRAINING

Toilet-training

Don't worry about it, the Akita will do it all on its own. The first phone call we get from new owners to tell us how the dog is settling in, always includes the words "and he hasn't done a thing in the house...". Akitas are naturally very clean animals. All you need to do is to observe one simple rule: always put your puppy outside after it has woken up or after it has been feeding or drinking. The "big job" habit will fall into a pattern within a couple of days, and so you will soon know when the dog needs to go out.

Lead

This is the fun one. Have you ever seen a bucking bronco? You soon will, the moment you first put a youngster on the lead. This will spark off such leaps and bounds as you have never seen before. But remember, you have to win this battle. So go to it, always making sure you are kind and firm — and don't forget that titbit for the reward. It will take a few days to bring your Akita under control, but you will get there.

Time schedule

If you get up at 7.00 a.m. and retire to bed at 11.00 at night, teach your Akita to respect these times. Arrange feeding and exercise to fit in with your schedule, and keep to regular times. If your puppy cries or howls before 7.00 a.m., try not to listen. A couple of days will sort it out. Your heart-strings will be stretched to the limit, but if you give in you will be up at whatever hour your puppy chooses. It will learn your schedule very quickly, and what a greeting you will get when you do appear!

Akita puppies are full of fun, they are also very strong. This pup can already manage to hold a pint pot in its jaws

UNDERSTANDING

Your puppy's character and temperament is partly hereditary and partly waiting to be moulded by you. You must watch your puppy and learn its natural ways so that you can work out how to teach it the manners and understanding that you wish it to have. It is a matter of learning their language. Akita puppies are very intelligent, more so than most breeds at an equivalent age. They will learn words from as early as four weeks old; and from eight weeks onwards they will have a growing intelligence comparable to that of a much more mature dog in other breeds. You should take this opportunity to teach your Akita as much as possible. You will never exhaust its quest for knowledge.

This chapter has, perhaps been a little serious. But your new puppy is very precious, not only to you, but to the future of the breed. It is important that you understand the serious task of rearing your youngster, as well as being able to enjoy him. We do not need to write about all the fun you will have with your Akita — for you have the best teacher in the world!

CHAPTER THIRTEEN

AKITAS IN THE SHOW RING

THE exhibition of pedigree dogs is a most pleasurable hobby for many people. Some have just one good quality animal, which they show occasionally. Others become deeply involved and exhibit large numbers of dogs. They usually breed their dogs and remain in the sport for many years. There is no doubt that if you are looking for a striking show dog, the Japanese Akita is a wonderful choice. It looks very beautiful, and its size and presence serve it well in the exhibition ring. However, the glory of winning should not be the ultimate goal. If you are exhibiting a good specimen of the breed, which you have either bred or purchased, it should be because you want confirmation from knowledgeable judges that you have a superb Akita. The real purpose of exhibition is to discover the best animals, so that they can be selected as the best breeding stock to produce the next generation.

However, we would not be human if we did not strive to enhance our dog's qualities by presentation, grooming and expertise of handling. This is not as trivial as it sounds. It is important that the best dogs are presented and handled to the best of our ability in order that the judge can properly assess them. He is not going to appreciate the finer points of conformation if he is faced with a dirty, overweight, badly behaved specimen. There is a certain expertise involved in being a good exhibitor, and you should always do your best to show off your dog's qualities and reduce the chance of the judge being unable to make a proper assessment. That aside, for the true doggy person, there is a great deal of pleasure in bathing the dog, grooming it and learning to handle it, so that when you enter the ring you can be proud of the noble, striking animal that the Akita is. There are many skills to acquire, and at our kennels we have mostly learnt the hard way, through trial and error and dedicated hard work.

If you become a regular showgoer, you will make many friends, but you will also make some enemies. These are the people who are unable to make an honest assessment of their dog and they envy anyone else their success. It is a highly regrettable side of showing, but as with all forms of competition it is inevitable. The best thing to do is to ignore any unpleasantness, and concentrate on your friends and fellow exhibitors who share the same sensible view as yourself.

It is difficult to decide how much encouragement should be given to new Akita owners as to whether they should show their dog. Some breeders like to think that every animal that comes from their kennel is of show quality. In our view, you should always be honest about the quality of any Akita. Of course, you cannot say to someone: "Do not show your dog." But if someone asks your opinion, you should give it, without worrying about giving offence. For the exhibitor of a poor dog will not enjoy the rewards and pleasures that successful showing brings. It is far better for you to make an honest assessment of your dog and perhaps learn from this and purchase a better dog next time. You must also accept that dogs vary from day to day and, last Saturday's winner may not look so good this week. Judges will interpret things differently, you must accept the decision on the day. The only exception is if there is a genuine complaint of either dishonesty or incompetence. Thankfully, this is a rare occurrence.

We take great pride in our dogs and only ever exhibit good specimens presented to the best of our ability. There is no point in taking along an ungroomed and dirty exhibit which is badly handled. You must always give your dog the best chance possible to win the class, and there are many things you can do and practise so that your dog looks its best.

TRAINING

This begins the day you get your puppy. This should not be severe, pressure training, but simply opening up the channels of communication — a mixture of love and play coupled, with teaching the puppy to follow your lead. For instance, if you are planning to show your dog, it will have to stand in a ring — so don't teach it to sit. All play should be related, in some form or other, to the show ring. In that way, showing will be a pleasure to your Akita and not a chore. Too much training will result in your Akita becoming bored. It learns quickly and does not require endless repetition. You do not need to teach proper ringcraft until the puppy is perhaps five months of age. Let it grow up and enjoy doing the things puppies do. When you do begin, lessons should be of a repetitive nature and the rewards should be great.

We never use "bait"; we prefer to teach the dog to do our bidding, with a big cuddle as the reward. We find this works very well. It also has the advantage of ensuring that your dog stands still and is not wriggling around, looking for the food you have in your pocket. You will also avoid the horrible saliva which the dog will pass on to the judge's hands. You should train at home and, if you wish, at some of the excellent match meetings or ringcraft classes which are held all around the country. The idea is that you put your dog through the show ring procedure. Of course, you never know how your dog will behave when confronted with a ring full of other dogs; but if you have trained it well, your dog will at least be familiar with your commands. Many youngsters object quite strongly, by either sitting down or turning around, particularly when their teeth or rear end is being examined. Our training programme always includes a regular inspection of the teeth and handling around the rear and tail area, especially in young males. A visit from other "doggy" friends can also be used, so that your dog gets used to being handled by a stranger.

GROOMING AND PRESENTATION

You should always present a clean and shining dog for the judge's perusal. Bathing an Akita is not so difficult, and the dog dries relatively quickly. How often you bath is up to you. Bathing does not, in the main, spoil an Akita's coat. On the other hand, clever presentation can save you from this rather time-consuming and arduous task. We are often asked how we get our Akitas so clean and which shampoo we use. The answer is not in the make of shampoo; it is a matter of management. No amount of shampoo will turn an Akita who has been dirty for the past month, into a gleaming show dog. You have to administer the care and cleaning on a daily basis. There are many excellent shampoos on the market and most people have their particular preferences.

Once you have bathed your dog, it will need a thorough grooming. You can use whichever brushes and combs you prefer to give your Akita that gleaming, plushy coat, which is so typical of the breed. The Kennel Club rules that no preparations can be used on the coat which will still be present when the dog is being exhibited; so care has to be taken in your choice of sprays, chalk and other aids. We do not use any of these devices, because we believe that you can't beat soap and water. It's cheaper too!

When you are at a show, it is always worthwhile giving a final grooming before entering your class. Sitting around in the car and on the show bench will "unplace" the dog's coat, so an inspection and brush-up will help to correct this. We like to take ourselves off to a quiet place, where the dog is not distracted, to administer this final preparation.

HANDLING

Again, this is a very personal matter. You see people who run with dogs that are on yards of leads which they wrap around their hands. Others have a rather vicious-looking choke chain. Some string up the dog's head when standing, and especially when moving.

We believe in gentleness. Even a dog as large and powerful as an Akita will appreciate gentle handling. There is nothing to be gained from dragging your dog around on the end of the lead, pulling and tugging violently. A very small signal from you, down the lead, to the dog, will elicit a response. We have our collars and leads specially made to fit each individual dog, selecting extra strong materials and clasps, which should be strong enough to hold the dog if the need ever arose. You should always use a strong lead and collar; for remember, this is a very powerful and fast animal that you are attempting to confine in a public place, probably surrounded by other young Akitas, including energetic males. But your choice of lead and collar should not hinder the line of the dog. The judge does not want to see the tackle you are using he wants to see the dog.

Exercise is important as the judge will be assessing the physical condition of the dog. Good muscle tone is required, especially in the rear quarters. Road-work is the best form of exercise for toning up slack muscles, but in many cases hard muscle tone or soft flabby muscles are hereditary. If your dog carries the hard tone, then it will save you a lot of walking. If not, you will have to rely on regular trotting exercise on a hard surface. In the early stages of training you should have established the correct speed at which to move your dog so that it displays the best possible gait. Don't copy other people. Every dog is different. Practice makes perfect, and in time you will find the correct pace for your dog. The chances are it will keep you fit as well!

When in the show ring, give yourself plenty of space, allowing for the size of the ring. Do not be crowded by other more aggressive handlers. Ensure you are properly in line and that the judge can see you. Courtesy should be observed at all times. It is clear from the breed standard what the judge is looking for, so it is important that you display your dog to show its proportions, its head, ear-set, coat-quality and the correct movement. Your handling technique should be used to ensure that the judge can fully appreciate your dog, while you keep control of the powerful animal you are exhibiting. Don't ever forget to praise your dog after the class, whether it wins or not. Remember, this should an an enjoyable day out for both of you.

CHAPTER FOURTEEN

JUDGING THE BREED

MOST people who breed more than one litter, or purchase several dogs of the same breed, are likely to get involved in the show world. They want to have their dogs judged by experts, and by the public at large. In theory, it is the dogs who conform most closely to the breed standard that will do well, and will be selected to perpetuate and improve the breed. In practice, there are many other factors, especially in these days when almost

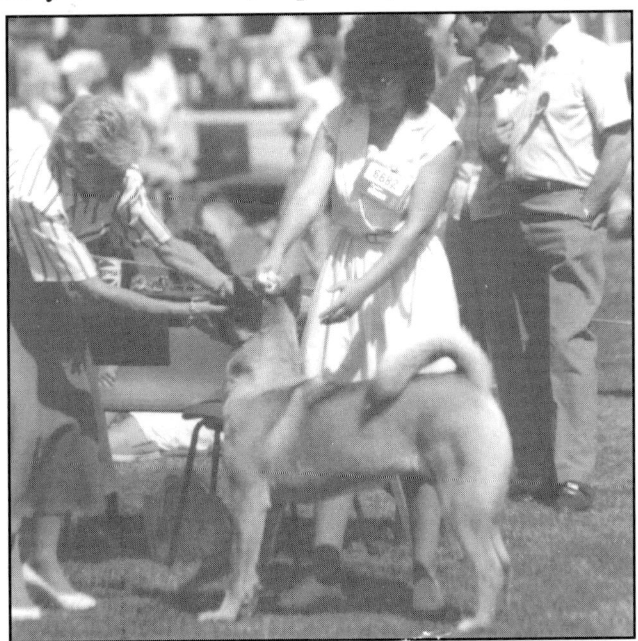

Mrs Joyce Mann, a highly respected judge, assesses Kiskas Kyoshi , owned by Karen and Steve Arme.

everybody wants to be a judge. They say that good judges are born, not made; and on the whole we would agree. For there are many good breeders of pedigree dogs who do not, for some strange reason, have the same ability when it comes to judging. Equally, there are some people that are excellent judges and can recognise supreme qualities in a dog, but cannot manage to produce those qualities in their own dogs. It all comes down to having an eye for a good dog. But this can be enhanced by experience and learning to recognise the fundamentals of a dog's structure and soundness, as well as the major characteristics of a particular breed.

If you become a judge, you should be aware of the huge responsibility you have taken on, and be assiduous in the way you exercise your power. Many breeding decisions are made upon a dog's show wins, and so the first priority must be to select animals that visually represent the breed. They must carry the fundamentals of the breed and be sound of mind and body. They will all have faults; and these must be judged depending on what is most harmful to that particular breed. It is vital that you are fully conversant with the breed standard and that you have an interest in the breed. There is nothing worse than reading comments in judges' critiques which are in total conflict with the demands of the standard.

In order to be a good judge, you must be completely objective. As far as you are concerned, there are no politics in the show ring. There are just dogs; not people, not views or fancies, not your ideas or their ideas — just dogs. You are not looking for your "type" of Akita, which you feel conforms best to the standard, or their "type", which they feel conforms best to the standard; you are there to look at dogs, just dogs. They are all trying to conform to the standard — and there is only one standard. It is this standard that you should be carrying in your head each time you step into that exhibition ring as a judge.

It is true to say that you get better at judging the more you do it. The more you see, the more you learn, and it becomes easier to accept that Mrs Blogg's type, which is quite different from your own, still represents the breed very well. You can't please everybody, but you must be confident that you did your best and that you know the reason for your selections. You can therefore answer any criticism with a truthful account of your decisions of the day. It is important to remember that you are being asked to judge on a particular day; for dogs like humans have off days. You should not be influenced by what has gone before.

Your conduct in the judging ring is most important. You should always be courteous to the handlers and kind to the dogs. You should give every dog, good or not so good, the best possible chance, and consider its virtues against its faults. You are looking for the best Akita, but this should be a pleasurable experience for all concerned. Enjoy the animals, and remember, they should be praised and loved, no matter how they look. They will have given their all in the ring, without knowing if they looked good or bad.

One of the greatest dangers is to judge on comparison. Of course you must compare the dogs in the ring who are competing against each other. But you are there to compare each one of those dogs to the breed standard and not to its neighbours. When you have assessed each dog individually against the standard, you will know which dog conforms most closely, and therefore you have your selection. You should never say: "That dog was better than that one." That is not a good enough reason. All dogs should be judged in comparison with the breed standard which is carried in your head.

This is summed up by an episode that happened some years ago to a novice judge who gave first prize in a puppy class. The choice was justified because "the puppy looked fine, well grown and mature and was showing far better and in better coat than the rest." Yes, the dog was mature, in full bloom and showing its head off; but there were at least three other puppies in the class who were not quite so well grown, not in such full coat and that fidgeted a bit when being assessed. But they were far superior in the most important points of the breed standard, and should certainly have beaten the winning dog. When the novice judge thought about it, he did agree. He also agreed that he had learned something...for the next time.

We have judged in many countries. Some are more strict than others. Some dogs are good, some bad — all are there to be assessed by you. You must always be clear in your mind that you are judging the dogs in front of you as representatives of their breed. It does not matter who is on the other end of the lead, which dog won last week, or which is a champion. It does not matter what other, less knowledgeable people will say about your placings. It *does* matter that you give every dog the benefit of your expertise and knowledge of the breed. Equally, you must never be afraid to question your own decisions afterwards. You should analyse your placings, in case you missed anything at the time, and so you can learn something for the next time.

We adopt a certain procedure which, when carried out with mental reference to the breed standard, serves very well as an assessment of each dog. In this instance, we have applied it specifically to the Akita and its breed standard.

1. Allow the dog to stand four-square, in an open space, in a profile position.

2. Visually assess the general appearance and overall balance, taking note of the dog's total presentation. What you are looking for is a level topline, correct height, correct length of leg, set of tail and carriage, arch of neck, set of ear, depth of muzzle, stop, lay of shoulder, strength of pasterns, depth of brisket, medium tuck-up, hind angulation, condition of feet, coat quality, colour and presentation.
3. View the dog from the front to determine that he is parallel and that neither the elbows or feet turn in or out. Shoulders should be firm and parallel. Chest deep and broad, but not wide or narrow. The neck should be thick.
4. View the dog from the rear to determine that the hindquarters appear strong. Hindlegs should be parallel, with no suggestion of weak or cow hocks. Feet should point straight ahead. Rump should be strong and firm, and not narrow.
5. Move to the front and stand well back.View the overall expression in the head. Dogs should appear masculine but not coarse, bitches should be pretty but not fine. The head should appear as a blunt triangle with a clearly defined stop, and the muzzle should be strong and deep. Appearance should be of keen alertness and strength.
6. Approach the dog from the front (so that it can see you and accept your advances). Examine the head. The skull should be flat, forehead broad and there should be a pronounced stop. The muzzle should be broad and full. The proportions should be: nose to stop two parts; stop to occiput: three parts.

Feel that the ear is thick, rounded at the tip, wide at the base and correctly set on to the head; the ears should be neither too close together nor too wide apart. See that the eye is the correct almond shape; eyes should be moderately set apart, dark in colour with black rims. Check that no entropion or ectropion is present. Check that the jaws are strong, and that the teeth close in a scissor bite. Lips black, flews tight. View the head from the side to check that the muzzle is deep. Measure the ear for size by turning down the tip, which should just reach the upper eye rim. The full facial cheeks should complete the picture.
7. Examine the body, using both your eyes and your hands. Feel down the neck, which should be relatively short, arched and strong and should flow almost undetectably into the shoulders. Feel the withers and check the distance between the bones (ideally 2ins to 2½ins).

By placing the index finger of one hand on the withers and the index finger of the other hand on the most protruding bone at the top of the dog's front leg, the angle of shoulder can be both seen and felt. Check that the upper arm bone is of the right length to contribute to the proper forequarter angles. Feel the front legs to ensure the quality of bone. Check that the pasterns are almost vertical, and strong. Feet should be tight, with thick, resilient pads.

8. Feel that the chest is deep and reaches the elbow (although this may not be so in young stock). Place a hand on either side of the rib cage and press gently. The dog will exhale air from his lungs, thereby showing a good spring of rib.

9. Check the length of back, taking note of length of rib cage and length of loin. Back should be muscular, firm and level with no dipping behind the withers, and no rise or fall at the rump or fall-off at the croup. Tuck-up should be moderate, not saggy, and not tucked-up.

10. Feel the loins to determine that they are strong and not too short or too long. Feel at the thigh muscles, which should be well developed and in hard condition. Check that there is a good second thigh. Feel the stifle. This should not be straight or over-angulated. Check that the patellas are firmly placed with no movement. Hocks should be well let down and firmly set, allowing no movement forward (i.e. an appearance of double-jointedness, commonly called "popping hocks").

11. If the dog is a male, check that both testicles are fully descended.

12. Check the set of tail on to the back. The base should be wide and the tail should be drawn down to measure, reaching just to the hock. The tail may be curled either left or right or full circle, but must always be carried to fall either to, or below, the level of the back. An uncurled, or sickle tail, would be considered a serious fault in all countries.

13. Feel that the dog has a wealth of undercoat and that the top coat is standing straight away from the body, with a plushy appearance. The top coat should be harsh, not coarse, and the texture can be felt by rubbing the hair between the fingers. There should be no suggestion of feathering on ears, trousers, skirts, hocks or feet. Consider the colouring: is it a definite colour, if it has markings, are they clear, and do the colour and markings conform to the standard?

14. To assess that the dog moves with the correct Akita gait, send him away from you in a straight line. The hindlegs should be parallel and powerful, not stilted (moving just up and down), nor driving fiercely. The dog should return on the same line. The front should be parallel, with firm pasterns, giving strength when the feet meet the ground. The elbows should not turn in or out. There should be no sign of flapping or hackney-style movement. Move to the side and study the side gait. The strides should be of moderate length; the front positive, the rear firm. The massive weight of the dog should be carried along almost all at the same time, with a dignity and proudness. There should be no suggestion of

over-reaching in front with excessive long strides, or a terrific drive or a stilted powerless action behind. The topline must remain level at all times. There should be no weakness of back and no change in tail carriage. The trot is brisk and agile, suggesting that movement is no encumbrance to the dog.

15. By now you will have already tested the temperament of the Akita. It should be ready to accept you, and the surroundings. He should stand firm beneath your touch and remain alert. He should not display any aggression or intolerance of your actions. He should not back off. It is important that you respect the Akita's natural guarding instinct. You must remember that you are the trespasser, and the dog is with its trusted owner and companion. You must always display your intentions and approach the dog from where he can see you and be able to note your intentions. You must not show fear or nervousness, for he will sense it. You must always be aware of his power and speed.

16. By carrying the written standard in your mind, you should be able to assess your findings in direct comparison with what the standard requires.

CHAPTER FIFTEEN

SPREADING THE WORD

THE journey from mid-California across the desert to Santa Barbara on the coast, takes about four hours by car, and you will be lucky to see another living creature. It is just mile after mile of desert covered with scrub, until at last, you round the final bend to see a beautiful, cool lake. Those pioneers of the old days were certainly made of tough stuff. For pioneering, in any sense, is very hard. And so it is with breeding and developing a new breed of dog. The road is long and hard and there are many treacherous encounters along the way; there are many disappointments and moments of despair. There are times when you think everything is going smoothly, and then crash! — you have gone forward two paces and gone back one. There are so many unknowns when you are working with dogs that may have a pedigree on paper, but you do not know those dogs personally and you have not seen their relatives. You will have to rely on the people who sold you your initial stock, and, if you are shrewd, you will instigate your own separate investigations.

We believe the only way to develop a distinctive line within a breed is to select a number of initial animals within a small number of chosen lines. You can then select from the animals they produce which of them should go forward for future breeding. The prerequisite is that you are absolutely honest in your assessment. You must look at each dog's qualities and faults. You must acknowledge their known hereditary problem traits, and be ready to deal with them when they appear, as they inevitably will. You must keep your counsel and not become disheartened by criticism. It takes time to produce good-quality dogs from mixed origins and you will not get it right at the first attempt, or in your first generation. You will probably not get it right in the next generation...but in time, you will. If you have selected carefully, the second generation will be closer to the mark, and this gives you something to build on. The progress may not be easy to see the for outsider, but you and other genuine fanciers will appreciate your work. When a true Akita fancier looks at your stock, they will be able to see the pattern which you are striving to create. These are the people you should listen to if you are bogged down with a particular problem, or have become too elated at producing a top winner. An outsider's view can restore calm and commonsense. Pioneers must have patience, resolution and total commitment to the future well-being of the breed.

We imported six original Akitas, all from the same line in some respects, but with influences from three others. The first four, which arrived close together, consisted of two puppy bitches and two adult males. The plan was, in the first instance, to breed the first puppy bitch to the first male and the second puppy bitch to the second male. The second male would then be bred to the first bitch, and a male produced from the first mating would perhaps be bred to the second imported puppy bitch. We hoped that the puppies produced from these initial matings would give us a good idea of the over-riding qualities and faults, and what regions these came from. However, the first bitch puppy broke her leg and so a mating had to be postponed. Then the first male turned out to be sterile.

Plan A was not to be; but Plan B worked out very well, producing a lovely litter with many qualities and very few problems. In the meantime Plan C was put into operation, with the first bitch being mated to the second dog. At the time, we felt that we were putting the cart before the horse, but someone was on our side, for the resulting litter was lovely — distinctively Akita, large, colourful and with good temperaments. However, some problems were present, and these had to be assessed and dealt with. A repeat mating produced a similar litter and so, to a certain extent, proved what was present in the lines and in that particular combination. A close assessment of these early puppies highlighted the problems - the qualities appeared to be pretty static —and so we decided to import again.

This time we chose a bitch in whelp. She was closely related to our first imports and she had been mated to a dog of our choice. This was an attempt to eliminate the faults and reinforce the qualities we were producing in our stock. We were very fortunate that our friends in California allowed us to "loan" the bitch, for they did not wish to part with her. She arrived in the UK and had her puppies in quarantine. She produced a lovely litter, and we were thrilled. But alas, at five weeks of age the puppies became sick. After two weeks of continuous nursing, day and night, we saved six and lost one. It was later discovered that parvovirus was the cause of the trouble.

We were not pioneering the breed to make money, but the combined cost of shipping the bitch, the whelping-down, the kennelling and the vet's bill was punitive. However, the experience gained was enormous, and that was without knowing that our chosen puppy from the litter would be the first Akita to win a group at a championship dog show, as well as being a much-loved pet. Later assessment of the stock also gave us invaluable information about those particular lines.

As time went on, we discovered that a particular combination produced certain problems, and so, very reluctantly, we decided to abandon one of our foundation lines. It was not an easy decision to make but then we didn't expect things to be easy. If you are pioneering, you have to be prepared to admit when you have made mistakes. We assessed the rest of our stock and ear-marked those that possessed the qualities we had so admired in our "abandoned" line. We then pursued a breeding programme using these individuals. It took longer, but it proved to be a safer route. We did not give up, for we knew what we wanted. It was in those lines somewhere — all we needed was the key.

Our very first litter gave us a most notable dog puppy. He was truly an Akita in every respect. He went out into the show world and, in his own inimitable style, he won the hearts of many and became a great ambassador for the breed. We loved him dearly, and we looked forward to the day when he would sire puppies of his own. You can imagine how devastated we were when, at only eighteen months of age, we lost him. He died from bone cancer. He never became a sire, and so we shall never know what he would have given to the breed — perhaps a lot, perhaps nothing. It is something we still wonder about.

We took note of other Akitas that were being bred in the UK. We were scanning for a possible outcross: a dog that was not connected to our line but which possessed certain qualities that we were seeking. We also kept track of puppies we had produced, which were now being used for breeding. Some problems which appeared did confirm our decision to abandon that first line. By this time we were reasonably pleased with the stock we were producing. They all had the breed's distinctive characteristics, but there were some things which we needed to improve. We looked at the males which were available in the UK, and after careful analysis, we decided to look abroad. This implied no criticism of the Akitas in this country, but we were looking for something very specific. We now understood many aspects of our original lines, and so we had a pretty good idea of what would work. Again, our thanks must go to those friends in California, for they allowed us to purchase a bitch that was related as an aunt to much of our original stock. After much deliberation, we decided to mate her to a Canadian dog that carried the qualities we were looking for. There was the additional bonus that he had a sprinkling of the old Japanese blood.

The plan was simple. We would take this dog, mate him to our "aunt" (who had proved to be less dominant than her mates in her previous litters) and, hopefully, we would produce puppies with the sire's dominant qualities but retaining the qualities of our own stock through the dam. We were aware of the danger of the sire introducing faults to our line, but you have to be prepared to take a calculated risk. You will never find the perfect mate, and as long as you are not risking a fault which could prove harmful to the puppies, it is acceptable. Our "aunt" came into quarantine and produced her litter, though our luck ran true to form, with an expensive trip to the vet for a caesarian section as part of the proceedings. At the end of all this, the puppies looked very mediocre. They were dull and dismal, and not particularly big or strong either. We were very disappointed, for things seemed to be getting more difficult as time went on. Our misfortunes had included a broken leg, a sterile male, parvo-virus, and now a disappointing litter. Surely, we were due a break.

As is so often the case, the answer lay in patience. The puppies' development was not as we had expected, and they grew beautiful, displaying many of the qualities we had been seeking. In fact, they blossomed into good Akitas — and we had learnt another lesson; puppies from different lines develop differently. When they were old enough to use for breeding, we chose our brilliant red male, who had good feet, superb action, a deep body and a calm temperament. The plan was to mate him to our second import bitch, now proven as our best producer, and then mate one of the resulting bitch puppies back to one of the males produced earlier. This time, we got our lucky break — and it was certainly worth waiting for. It was the kind of surprise that makes pioneering so worthwhile. For instead of having to wait for another generation, we came up trumps at the first attempt. The litter by our red dog had virtually all the qualities we wanted. We estimated that we were 75 per cent of the way there. Now all we had to do was to nurture the puppies, and pray that they developed well. We chose our male, the one that was to lead us into the future, and redoubled our prayers that he would not be carrying any unknown genes that would pass on faults to his offspring.

This time, our prayers were answered. He grew into a beautiful Akita and has been admired the world over for his qualities and temperament. He is proving to be a good sire, passing on many of his qualities to his offspring, and it is his son that will be taking us into the Nineties.

Good pioneers probably never reach their ultimate goal; they are

Kyphox Buzz of Kiskas: pictured with Kath Mitchell and judge Bob Gregory after winning Best of Breed at the 1989 Belfast Championship Show. The dog was bred by Louise Gadella.

constantly striving to improve the quality of their dogs. And these are the people to admire for their tireless hard work and dedication. We have experimented by making two more selected male outcrosses, and we have been very pleased with the results. We have sent many of our dogs abroad, which will hopefully help breeders to find and improve their own lines. We have also kept a close check on litters being produced in the UK that have been sired by our dog or produced out of bitches we have bred, for we are always on the look-out for a puppy that might strengthen our line. In fact, this was how we got hold of our latest star, who was produced by a young breeder. This dog proves that you should never be kennel-blind when you are developing a breed. You should always be able to recognise something good in someone else's plan.

As the breed develops, it is not always the genuine pioneers that are acknowledged. A superb animal may be produced by a newcomer to the breed, but this is probably the result of a plan set in motion long before by the original pioneers and only coming to fruition now. You cannot say that you have a line, unless you have developed one which is distinctive within the breed. A kennel affix is not, and never can be, a passport to a certain kind of dog, unless it is backed up by a dog which is recognisably from that kennel. You cannot claim to be a true pioneer, unless you have pioneered with a plan, and a goal, which you have achieved.

CHAPTER SIXTEEN

HEALTH

AS with all breeds of dog, there are certain problems related to physique, heredity and general health. The Akita is no exception, and although it does come a long way down the scale when compared with many other breeds, it is important that such matters are taken into consideration by present and prospective owners. The problems may divert from the ideal type or they may cause harm or discomfort to the dog. We list here, in no particular order, some of the things which can occur in the Akita. We do not suggest that you dwell on these things, for they are, in the main, unfortunate occurrences; but nevertheless, they can be present in any Akita, and if we respect the fact that they do exist, we will more ready to make an attempt to eliminate them.

PROGRESSIVE RETINAL ATROPHY

Commonly known as PRA, this is a condition of the eye which eventually causes blindness. It is known to be hereditary and therefore care should be taken when breeding to ensure that the disease is not passed on. There are simple and painless tests which can be carried out by a specially qualified veterinary surgeon. It is recommended that the dog should be tested each year until it is about six years old, before it can be stated with absolute certainty that there is no problem.

The problem is that most dogs and bitches will be used for breeding before the age of six and so, to some degree, the initial tests only give a guide. However, they are the best way forward and it is important that they are done. Thankfully, the disease is not common in the Akita, as it is in some other breeds, and a watchful approach will hopefully keep it at bay.

HIP DYSPLASIA

This condition is well-known in the Akita, but fortunately it is not common. It is a very complex subject and many eminent vets have made studies of it. The problem with H.D. is that it can be caused by a variety of factors, both singly and in combination. The hereditary factor is quite strong, but it seems to be multifactorial in many cases: the rearing of puppies, environmental conditions and injuries can all contribute. It also appears that dogs with bad hip joints will often produce dogs with bad hip joints. Unfortunately, it does not follow that dogs with good hip joints always produce dogs with good hip joints. However, dogs which are structurally sound in hip joints will, as with any other structural pattern, be a better bet for producing future offspring with structurally sound hip joints.

True hip dysplasia will eventually cause great pain to the dog and will render it lame. There are X-ray schemes available which offer a scoring chart. The X-ray plates are examined by qualified people who measure and check the fitments of the various hip bones and tendons; they then offer their analysis of degree in numbers. The lower the variation from the perfect, the lower the "hip score". Again, it is recommended that you have your Akita X-rayed after it has reached the age of twelve months, and then have the plates assessed by someone who is well qualified in that area. It is important to remember that the Akita is not fully developed until it is about three years of age, and so you will have to wait until then to get a true picture. But any X-rays taken prior to this should give a good guide to the finished hips.

ENTROPION

This is a common problem in Akitas and it would be fair to say that it is found in most breeding lines. The condition is a turning-in of the eye rim, which causes great discomfort to the dog as the eye lashes rub upon the eye. In severe cases this can lead to blindness, as the lashes scrape the surface of the cornea. Sometimes the condition will appear in puppies in their first weeks, but sometimes it will not appear until the dog is much older, perhaps over twelve months.

Several things can cause the condition, such as too much flesh around the eye area, bone structure or too long a lid. It is definitely hereditary and can either appear in immediate offspring or crop up a few generations later. The condition can be easily corrected by surgery, and this should be done for the comfort of the dog. However, this will not alter the fact that the affected dog or bitch is carrying the problem.

ECTROPION

This is the opposite of entropion: the bottom eye-lid is too loose, and turns outward and downward. Apart from being unsightly it does not cause as much discomfort, except that dirt will collect and will eventually cause infection.

SKIN

The Japanese Akita does suffer more than many other breeds from various skin complaints. No-one has, as yet, come up with a cure for any of them. The nappy-rash syndrome appears in many youngsters, and a similar problem can occur later on, very often with each coat-cast. More severe conditions need antibiotics, but these only alleviate the discomfort and do not cure the problem. Any skin disorder will be fairly complex, and should only be dealt with after taking advice from those knowledgeable within the breed or from your veterinary surgeon. Skin should be checked regularly and any problems should should be dealt with immediately.

BONES

There are several conditions of bone formation problems which can occur in large breeds of dogs. The Akita has, to some degree, suffered from growth plate problems, Osteochondrosis; a problem with the development of joint cartilage, too much calcium, and an inability to absorb calcium. Most bone problems are being investigated by the experts, and their advice should be sought via your own veterinary surgeon if you suspect a problem.

SLIPPING PATELLA

A problem found fairly often, but rarely admitted. This is the slipping-off of the dog's knee-cap. It can be caused by various things — too loose a ligament or too shallow a groove in the bone holding the knee-cap. It does not always cause distress, but it is hereditary to some degree. Injury can bring on the problem. If it is found, investigations should be undertaken to establish the cause, and the advice of your veterinary surgeon or a specialist should always be sought. One of the great dangers is to have too straight a stifle in the Akita.This can so often cause the patella to move and so produce unsoundness.

HOCKS

"Popping hocks" are found in the Akita, and is seemingly more prevalent in some bloodlines. The hock joint is somewhat unfirm and a double-jointed type condition can be seen. The hock, if pressed from the rear, will move forward. This condition should be taken account of when breeding and judging, as it is detracts from the strength you would wish to see in a dog as heavy and substantial as the Akita.

THE CRUCIATE LIGAMENT

The tearing or breaking of the cruciate ligaments in the rear legs is a problem that is found in many larger breeds, including the Akita. The experts say that it is not, in itself, hereditary, but it does seem that some dogs do have a pre-disposition to it. Therefore, in our opinion, any problem in this area should be carefully thought about when breeding. Surgery can be successful, and most veterinary surgeons can perform the operation. It is usually caused by injury, although sometimes just normal exercise can result in a break.

TORSION AND BLOAT

Most large, deep-chested breeds, are prone to torsion and bloat. Torsion is extremely painful, distressing, and most often fatal. It happens when the dog's stomach is full, and perhaps begins to swing, thereby causing an uneven distribution of the food and liquid and inviting the stomach or gut to twist. The gas then builds up and the dog is in extreme pain and in great shock. Immediate veterinary attention is required. You only have minutes in which to act.

Bloat is the general term for the large amount of gas which can be present in the gut. Your vet will have to release the gas and then administer surgery to remove the restriction. The animal will be in a state of shock when the vet administers the anaesthetic, and it is this that most often leads to a fatality. You should always monitor your feeding times and never exercise immediately after feeding. After exercise, the Akita should not be allowed to drink vast amounts of water to over-fill the stomach. The symptoms of bloat are: obvious discomfort, hard-blown belly, white foam at the mouth, and a look of distress. We cannot stress too much that you must react immediately to any of these signs.

PANCREAS AND LIVER DISORDERS

Disorders in these areas have occurred in the Akita, but no more so than in any other breed. The normal veterinary practices apply to Akitas.

INTUSSUSCEPTION

This is a "telescoping" of the intestine. It is generally in the small intestine, either higher up nearer to the stomach, or lower down nearer to the large intestine and so to the bowel. It generally appears with a colic condition and is brought on by the intestine constricting and the constricted section slipping into the larger (normal-sized) adjacent section, thereby forming a restriction. It occurs in all animals, usually in very young stock. In the case of dogs, it occurs in puppies, aged around twelve weeks. It has to be treated by surgery, but it is fairly easy to remedy if it is detected early enough.

The normal symptoms are for the puppy to vomit in a projectile manner or to produce a mucous-type excretion from the bowel. The puppy will appear unwell; and so any sign of an unhappy pup, coupled with the symptoms, should be investigated by your vet without delay.

WORMS

This is not really a problem so long as the normal treatments are given to puppies and, later on, to adults. The medicines that are available do a great job, but in our opinion they should be administered under veterinary supervision.

TRAVEL SICKNESS

Most Akitas travel extremely well. Some, thankfully a small number, never travel well at all. Many remedies have been tried, and most seem to fail. We have found that different dogs react better to different medicines, and so it is a matter of finding the right one to suit your Akita. Travelling in a safe, confined place is preferable to having a loose dog bouncing around in the back of the car. The excitement often results in sickness, and this can also be exacerbated by the owner fussing the dog and not allowing it to settle. It is a combination of the owner's and dog's behaviour that can cause the problem, rather than the motion of the car.

ANAESTHETIC

Akitas are strange animals in many ways and sometimes they do react unusually to anaesthetics. It is always worth mentioning to your vet that the Akita differs from other breeds in this respect, so that he can take extra care.

PAIN

Akitas do appear to have a high threshold for pain. On many occasions we have seen an Akita get up, wag its tail and walk about, just hours after a serious operation. This can mean that they are not displaying their true feelings of discomfort, and so we must be watchful in order to assess their true condition. Your own special knowledge of the dog will often tell you more than the dog's actions.

HEALING

If an Akita is injured in any way, the dog will generally heal quite quickly. It has to be really ill before it will lie down, and this can cause problems. For instance, most dogs would not dream of walking on a cut pad but an Akita will try to carry on as normal. You must be firm and exert you authority when you know the dog needs to rest. Extra attention and affection from you will help during this difficult period.

INERTIA

This condition can occur in Akita bitches. It is strange that a bitch can have one or two litters quite easily and then suffer from Inertia with a subsequent litter. She may then go on to have another litter and experience no further problems. It is not easy to recognise Inertia, as whelping is so often a calm and steady affair. However, a watchful eye, coupled with your own knowledge of your bitch should set alarm bells ringing. Don't leave it to chance; if you suspect anything, contact your vet.

MASTITIS

Akita bitches produce vast amounts of milk for their puppies. It is important that this milk is kept flowing to ensure that it does not congeal, not just because of the milk, but because the mammary area can be prone to inflammation or infection. This can quickly lead to mastitis. Both teats and nipples should be inspected regularly to ensure they remain supple and show no sign of infection. If mastitis does develop it can easily lead to septicaemia (blood poisoning), which does endanger the life of the mother.

ECLAMPSIA

This is sometimes called 'milk fever', and it is an extremely dangerous condition for the Akita mother. It occurs when the body does not produce enough calcium to cover the needs of the bitch, or rather, the body fails to ensure that the calcium is properly used. Supplementation of calcium is not enough: the bitch will need special treatment from your vet. The new mother should be watched over carefully, and any signs of shaking, unsteadiness or excessive saliva should be immediately reported. Sometimes hormonal changes can give rise to similar symptoms, but you should always refer to your vet immediately. As with torsion and bloat, you only have minutes to act.

MONORCHIDS AND CRYPTORCHIDS

It has been medically proved that males with no testicles will, if bred from, produce no offspring. Males with only one testicle may well breed normally, but the retained testicle will be infertile and the offspring will carry infertility problems. It is recorded that around 80 per cent of retained testicles become cancerous and therefore will endanger the dog's life. It is easy to appreciate the problems that would result from breeding with a male that is not entire; but it must also be appreciated that a retained testicle is a hazard to health and must be treated by surgery.

V.K.H

The V.K.H. syndrome, or Haradas disease has been found in the Akita. It is a most distressing disease causing tremendous discomfort to the dog, and it leads to eventual blindness and other handicaps. It is linked to auto-immune problems, skin complaints and eye disorders, and is very complex, with little being known about its origins or a possible cure. Several Akitas in the UK have been diagnosed with the disease and all information is being held by Dr Keith Barnet at the Animal Health Trust at Newmarket. The early symptoms could indicate other problems, but later symptoms which could indicate V.K.H. are: cloudy eyes, red eyes, whitening of the hair around the eyes and muzzle, severe irritation, hair loss. Nervous signs include: going round in circles, head tilt and change in normal behaviour. There could be a loss of pigment around the nose and eyes and a suggestion of blindness. The symptoms are always bi-lateral (equally affecrting both sides of the body — and so both eyes are always affected). Due to the rarity of the disease, many vets might not diagnose V.K.H., and so if you suspect there is a problem your Akita should be referred direct to Newmarket.

LONG COATS

The gene which produces a long coat is present in the Akita. Puppies are still produced with a long coat, with feathering on the ears and legs. It is no hardship to the dog; indeed some think it rather beautiful. Akitas with these coats are not suitable for exhibition, but they make super pets.

DROP EARS

Again, the gene is present, and these dogs are not suitable for showing, although they are true Akitas in every other respect and make good pets. It would generally be agreed that you should not breed from Akitas which carry a long coat and/or drop ears.

CHAPTER SEVENTEEN

BREED ACHIEVEMENTS IN THE U.K.

SINCE the Akita arrived in the UK it has achieved a number of notable firsts in the show ring, and in other areas.

1983

FIRST AKITA TO WIN A PUPPY STAKES ROUND AT A GENERAL CHAMPIONSHIP SHOW
KOSHO KI'S KIMONO OF KISKAS (pictured above),
Darlington, September 1983
She was also the first Akita to win Best Puppy in Show at a Championship Show, when she took honours at the B.U.B.A. the same

year. There were no particular successes at this specialist show again until 1987, when Wendy and Spencer Bell's puppy dog KYSAMI KEISATU (above) went reserve Best Puppy in Show.

1984

FIRST BEST IN SHOW AT AN ALL-BREED VARIETY SHOW
ARROWCREEKS REDMAN OF FIRE
Bebington Limit Show, April 8th, 1984
Owners: Pieter and Helen Burke.

FIRST P.A.T. DOG
TEGWANI AMANA AT FRATTON (above)
Owner: Mrs Jacqui Jones
The first Akita to actively work as a PRO DOGS P.A.T. dog: she spent many days visiting patients in hospital.

FIRST AKITA TO ENTER POLICE DOG TRAINING
A young Akita male, bred by Mrs Beryl Mason, entered the London Metropolitan Police Dog Centre and, under the supervision of Chief Inspector Clarke stayed for 12 months. Unfortunately the dog did not meet the very high standards set by the school and was returned to his owner.

1985

FIRST BEST PUPPY IN SHOW AWARD AT A GENERAL ALL-BREEDS CHAMPIONSHIP SHOW.
KISKAS MADAME BUTTERFLY (above)
Scottish Kennel Club Championship Show, May, 1985.

FIRST "TRIPLE" AWARD AT A GENERAL ALL-BREEDS CHAMPIONSHIP SHOW
KISKAS YUM YUM (above)
Blackpool, June 1985
Best A.V. Not Separately Classified, winner of the Puppy Bitch Stakes Round and also the Utility Group Best Puppy. Interesting to note that she was full litter sister to MADAME BUTTERFLY.
Owners: Brian & Brenda Pearson and Kathryn Pearson-Smith.

FIRST QUALIFYING FINALIST OF THE SPILLERS/DOG WORLD PUP OF THE YEAR COMPETITION.
KISKAS TRIAD (above)
Having won three rounds, and eventually taking the ultimate qualifying award at a major Championship show, Kiskas Triad became the first and, so far, the only Japanese Akita to take part in this prestigious final, confined to the top puppy stakes winners at the previous year's championship shows.

FIRST ENTRY INTO THE INTERNATIONAL JUNIOR HANDLING COMPETITION
VOODOO DOLL OF KISKAS
Young Janette Bridgwood, a keen handler of dogs, entered the classes held around the country in an attempt to qualify for the national Best Junior Handler title. She was successful in the first round and went on to compete in the finals at Richmond Championship Show in September 1984, where there was a tremendous entry of five hundred dogs in twelve groups. Janette came out top and went on to the finals at the Hotel Metropole, Birmingham, in January 1985. She handled her own dog and then had to handle a strange dog during the competition against eleven other handlers. Once more round the ring and she gained the title Junior Handler of the Year for the UK. This meant that Janette had to compete in the world finals at Crufts in the following February. As all the other competitors were coming from abroad and could not handle their own dogs, Janette was not allowed to handle her own dog. So she chose an Akita, Voodoo Doll of Kiskas, and after a splendid effort, Janette (pictured above with Voodoo Doll) was judged third in the world.

1986

FIRST JUNIOR WARRANT WINNER IN THE JAPANESE AKITA BREED

TELDALE TABASCO AT FARMBROOK (above)

September 1986

Owners: Chris and Sue Thomas.

The dog was aged 12 months and five days at the time of his win.

FIRST GROUP WIN AT A CHAMPIONSHIP SHOW
VOODOO DOLL OF KISKAS (above)
Paignton, July 1986
Handler: Geoff Corrish
Voodoo Doll later went to live with Joan and Uel Cooper in Ireland. In April 1988 Joan handled her to a another group win, this time at the Combined Canine Club's Championship Show in Southern Ireland. It came under the Irish classification for the breed, and so Akitas were judged in the Working Group.

1987

FIRST CLASSES SCHEDULED AT CRUFTS FOR THE JAPANESE AKITA
Prior to 1987, the Japanese Akita had to enter in the Not Classified classes, but this year there were twelve classes for the breed.

BEST OF BREED: KISKAS OMEN OF HOFFMAN (above)
Owners: Joan and Dave Rushby
BEST BITCH: NORTHERN HOPE AT VARENKA.
Owner: Mr Irene Rattray

FIRST DOUBLE TO BE WON AT A CHAMPIONSHIP SHOW
Bath, May 1987
BEST DOG: OVERHILLS HACKI-KO TAIPAN (above)

BEST BITCH: CHUJITSU OF OVERHILL AT SANJOSHA (above)
Owner: Mrs Pat Neil

A double of a different kind has been done no less than five times since that first one, namely by our dog, KISKAS KODIAK and his litter sister KISKAS TEICHO AT MAURAINE, owned by Maurice and Loraine Webb.

1988

DOG WORLD/PEDIGREE CHUM TOP RARE BREED AWARD
KISKAS KODAK (above)

This prestigious award was won by Kiskas Kodiak, who was Top Akita for the second year and gained more points than any of the other rare breeds. The presentation was made at Crufts. In 1989 Kodiak completed the triple by being judged Top Akita for the third year running.

FIRST RESERVE BEST IN CHAMPIONSHIP SHOW
KISKAS KODIAK

The Scottish Kennel Club's show in May 1988 saw Kiskas Kodiak winning his first group under judge Mrs Clare Coxall. He then went on to be judged Reserve Best in Show under Mr Jimmy Currie. Kodiak went on to win two more groups and two reserve groups at championship shows up to the end of 1989.

1989

FIRST ACHIEVEMENT IN WORKING TRIALS BY A JAPANESE AKITA

KISKAS OCELOT (pictured above jumping)

In March 1989, at the Yorkshire Working Trials Competition, Kiskas Ocelot, owned by Peggy Redfern-Smith, achieved his C.D.EX. He was trained by Peggy over a period of 18 months. He is still in training, and in November 1989 he qualified for his U.D. in Open, which is the first tracking stake.

WINNERS GO FORTH TO THE SUPERMATCH AND CONTEST OF CHAMPIONS.

Every year there are two competitions in the UK held to raise money for dog charities. The Supermatch in 1989 had two Japanese Akitas among its finalists, which are drawn from local canine societies' top dogs over the previous year. KUMAZAWA MISSISSIPPI, owned by Allison Goswey, and Trevor and Gill Rodgers' REDWITCH PAPER DOLL AT JILLTRAIN (above) both competed and were well supported on the night by many Akita fanciers.

The Contest of Champions is perhaps a grander affair, staged at a top London Hotel and boasting the country's top champions during the previous year. In April 1989 we were invited to take along KISKAS KODIAK, who had achieved his Top Rare Breed title in 1988.

FIRST AKITA ENTERED INTO OBEDIENCE COMPETITION.

NIGHTSTAR SAN BUCHI

Novice Class, November 12th, 1989

Owners: Joanne Madden and Peter Oxton

DOUBLE JUNIOR WARRANT
FARMBROOK LANDO CLARISSION AND SENSEI MIDSUMMER NIGHT'S DREAM (both pictured above)
The first sire, holding a Junior Warrant to produce a daughter, who also won a Junior Warrant
Owners: Paul and Margaret Shakespeare.
AKITAS IN AGILITY
CYPRUSHEE ARTFUL WILLIAM
Trained by Mrs Sheila Hart to cope with all aspects of agility, including the seesaw, jumps, weavy poles etc. He is now competing in general competition.
AKITAS IN THE RACING TEAM
Pieter and Helen Burke are the only people to own dogs that have taken part in carting races in the UK. Their team was mostly made up of Akitas with Arrowcreek's Redman Of Fire as the leader.

1990

FIRST CHALLENGE CERTIFICATES FOR AKITAS IN THE UK
Crufts, February 1990. Judge: Ken Bullock.
DOG CHALLENGE CERTIFICATE AND BEST OF BREED
AMERICAN CHAMPION TAMARLANE'S VENI VEDI VICI
UK owners: Marion Sargent and Mike Window.
Handler: Rusty Short, one of America's top professional handlers.

BITCH CHALLENGE CERTIFICATE AND FIRST BRITISH AKITA TO WIN A C.C.
KISKAS JEZEBEL
Owned and bred by Gerald and Kath Mitchell.
She is a granddaughter of our original import Kosho Ki's Kimono of Kiskas.

Winning line-up at Crufts: American Champion Tamarlane's Veni Vedi Vici (left) and Kiskas Jezebel.

Reserve Dog C.C.
KISKAS KODIAK
Owned and bred by Gerald and Kath Mitchell.

Reserve Bitch C.C.
FLASH DANCE AT VORMUND
Owners: John and Liz Dunhill.
Breeder: Mrs Ann Shimwell.

CHAPTER EIGHTEEN

THE WAY AHEAD

OWNERS of Japanese Akitas are captured not only by the beauty of the animal, but by its temperament and devotion to its human family. Unfortunately, it is a breed which is surrounded by a certain amount of controversy, possibly because of its striking beauty, coupled with its monetary value. It has achieved great status in the exhibition world and has been noted in several fields of work, both for its agility and for its temperament. It does seem destined to become even more popular in many countries of the world, and we sincerely hope that it can survive this mixed blessing.

In the short time the breed has been in the UK, we have seen a definite degeneration in some of its main characteristics and qualities. But we have also seen some very skilled breeders begin to develop a type that is truly worthy of its ancestry. There are those who are determined that the Akita will be able to fit into our society easily, yet still retain its original beauty and strength of character. There are, sadly, a few who appear to want nothing more than a full purse and will use the Akita to gain this profit.

The task ahead is a simple, if difficult, one. The Akita must remain as it is today. Those who are dedicated to its future must be steadfast and ensure that "any old Spitz dog" is not produced in place of the Akita. The Japanese Akita is a complex animal. It has to be bred and judged with care if it is to be preserved for the future. We fear that the breed is destined to travel through a period of mediocrity during its development, before all people realise that this dog must have the forward set of small, triangular ears, the noble crest of neck, the deep torso with level back, the high-flung tail, all covered in a brilliantly coloured and luxuriantly textured coat, to be a true Akita. When that realisation comes to pass, the way forward for the breed will be spectacular. It will have a future.

APPENDIX 1

GLOSSARY

ALMOND EYES: Almond-shaped by contour of surrounding tissue.
ANGULATION: Angles formed by lines and joints, particularly important in front and rear assemblies, shoulders, stifles, hock joints.
BACK: The part between withers and set-on of tail along vertebrae.
BALANCE: An overall, symmetrically proportioned dog in terms of size of parts, bone etc. in relation to each other.
BITE: Meeting of teeth when jaws are closed.
BLAZE: White or light-coloured streak down centre of head between eyes.
BRIDGE OF NOSE: Nasal bones extending from nostrils to stop.
CANINES: Two upper and two lower fang-like teeth just behind incisors.
CHEEK: Fleshy part of side of head below eyes; back and above mouth.
CHEST: Above brisket between shoulder-blades.
COLLAR: Marking around neck, usually white.
COW-HOCKED: Hock joints turn toward each other causing feet to turn out.
CREST: Upper arched portion of neck.
CROUP: Part of back above hindlegs and pelvis, in front of tail set.
DOUBLE COAT: Dual coat; short, soft undercoat with longer, coarser outer coat.
DOWN IN PASTERN: When weak or faulty joint tendons or muscles cause pronounced angulation at pastern and let foot down.
ELBOW: Joint between upper arm and forearm.
ELBOWS OUT: Turning out from body, not held close in.
EXPRESSION: Consists of appearance of eyes, surrounding tissue, ears, mouth and general head appearance.
FEATHERING: Longer hair fringe on ears, legs and tail.
FLEWS: Lips pendulous, particularly at inner corners.
FOREFACE: Muzzle in front of eyes.
FRONT: Forepart of body, forelegs, chest, brisket, shoulders.
FURROW: Medium line down centre of skull to stop.

HACKNEY ACTION: Picking up of front feet higher than necessary in motion.
HARSH COAT: Stiff and hard. Not coarse or wiry.
HEIGHT: Withers to ground measures shoulder height.
HOCKS WELL LET DOWN: When distance from hock-joint to ground is short (hocks to ground generally less than one third of height to hip).
LAYBACK OF SHOULDER: Scapula bone runs upward and backward from breastbone to backbone at an angle.
LOADED SHOULDERS: Over-development of shoulder muscles.
LOIN: Region on either side of vertebral column between last ribs and hindquarters.
LOW SET: Base of tail not on straight line with back; set lower or below level of topline.
LOWER THIGH: Stifle to hock. Sometimes referred to as second thigh.
MASK: Dark shading on foreface. May extend up to stop and across to cheeks.
MULTIFACTORIAL: When a condition is caused by more than one factor it would be described as being multifactorial.
MUZZLE: Foreface in front of eyes; nasal bone, nostrils and jaws.
OCCIPUT: Upper, back point of skull.
O.C.D.: Osteochondrosis, a problem affecting the development of joint cartilage. It can occur in any joint, but it is renowned for affecting specific parts of some particular joints. It is a multifactorial problem.
OUT AT ELBOWS: Elbows turn out from body in either stance or movement.
PADDLING: Moving with front feet wide.
PASTERN: Between foot and forearm leg bone.
PATELLA: A cap bone (similar to knee-cap) at stifle joint.
PRE-DISPOSITION: When an animal, in its make-up, is prone to any outside factor, or is likely to be affected by that factor.
QUALITY: An air of excellence, combining breed characteristics and including soundness and harmony, making the animal an outstanding specimen of the breed, both standing and in motion.
RACY: Long-legged, or comparatively slight build.
RANGY: Long-bodied, usually lacking depth in chest.
RUFF: Thick, longer hair growing around neck.
SCAPULA: Shoulder-blade.
SCISSOR BITE: Upper (incisor) teeth slightly projecting beyond lower teeth, fitting tightly like scissors.
SECOND THIGH: Stifle to hock. Sometimes referred to as lower thigh.
SHELLY: Narrow, shallow body lacking bone to balance size.

SHORT COUPLED: Short between last rib and hip joint forming short loins.
SICKLE TAIL: Carried out and upward in a semi-circle.
SKULL: Bony framework of head.
SNIPEY: Weak, pointed muzzle.
SOUNDNESS: Normal physical and mental health.
SPRING OF RIB: Degree of rib roundness and flexibility of rib cage to allow room for lungs and breathing.
STIFLE: Joint of hindleg, between thigh and second thigh.
STILTED: Choppy up and down gait. Upright shoulders, straight stifles.
STOP: Step-up from nose to skull. Indentation between eyes where nasal bone and skull meet.
STRAIGHT IN SHOULDER: Insufficient angulation (or lay-back) in scapula.
SUBSTANCE: Bone throughout.
TESTICLES: Two genital glands of the male.
THIGH: Hindquarters from hip joint to stifle.
TOPLINE: Backline from base of neck to base of tail.
TUCK-UP: Belly tucked up under loins. Waist.
TYPE: Characteristic qualities distinguishing breed. Embodiment of a standard's essentials.
WELL LET DOWN: Desirable degree of angulation of stifle and hock joints.
WITHERS: Peak of first dorsal vertebrae. Highest part of body just behind the neck.
WRINKLE; Loose-folding skin on forehead and/ or foreface.

APPENDIX 2

BREED CLUBS FOR THE JAPANESE AKITA AROUND THE WORLD

AUSTRALIA

The Akita Inu Club of Victoria
Secretary: Mrs. Glenys Stansfield,
63 English Street
Seville, Victoria 3139

BELGIUM

Club d'Akita Inus et races Japonaises Apparntees
Secretary: Mr.P. van den Cruyce, Kerkstraat 38
2190 Essen

CANADA

The Akita Club of Canada
c/o Bev Duncan
R.R. no.1
Orono, Ontario LOB 1MO

DENMARK

Spidshundeklubben
Leif Lehmann Jorgensen
Logstorvej 28
Ulbjerg, 8832 Skals.

FRANCE

Club Francais De L'Akita Inu
Secretariat: Sylvie Ghesquiere
Le Bas Fouillet
18220 AZY.

GERMANY

Akita-Club e.V.
Herrn Gerd-Lutz Lammers
Erlenkamp 26
4700 Hamm 1

NORWAY

Norsk Akita Klubb
Kari Loken
Stordamvn
13, 0671 Oslo 6

SCOTLAND

Japanese Akita Club of Scotland
Secretary: Mr Stuart Corrigan
22 Hill View Crescent
Glespin Lanark M11 0JE

SPAIN

Club Espanol de Perros Nordicos
Hermosilla
143, 1 dha -
28028 Madrid

SWEDEN

Rasklubb for Akita Inu
Ulla Grip
Fiskesa 2599
S - 76200 RIMBO

SWITZERLAND

Schweizerischer Klub for
Nordische Hunde Emmeng
Emmengasse 9
CH 4249 Blauen

UNITED KINGDOM

The Japanese Akita Club of Great Britain
Secretary: Mrs Kath Mitchell
Kiskas, Hillcroft
Mastin Moor
Chesterfield S43 3DH

The Japanese Akita Association
Secretary: Mr. Mike Window
Greenacres Boarding Kennels
Thurcaston Road
Leicester LE4 2QG

U.S.A.

The Akita Club of America
Secretary: Mrs. Sylvia Thomas
2155 Hackamore Place
Riverside
California 92506

APPENDIX 3

BRITISH KENNEL CLUB REGISTRATION FIGURES FOR THE JAPANESE AKITA

Year	Total number of dogs
1980	0
1981	1
1982	1
1983	14
1984	74
1985	131
1986	296
1987	421
1988	411
1989	711
TOTAL:..........................	2060

Total litters registered.....393

THE AKITA HOTLINE

The Hotline was set up to help Akita owners who had problems with their dogs, and to give general advice. The Hotline service, which is organised and run by the Japanese Akita Club of Great Britain, operates 24 hours a day.

SOUTH: 0707 260924

EAST: 0945 880377

WEST AND NORTH-WEST: 061 432 8913

NORTH AND NORTH-EAST: 0226 243826

MIDLANDS: 0246 472330

IRELAND: 0265 868253